GO TO JAIL
A CALL TO CHRISTIANS

BY

RICK BEZANSON

DEDICATION

This book is dedicated to our Lord Jesus Christ who took a very prodigal son and transformed him into a Reverend Doctor. All glory be to God and the Lamb forever! I also dedicate this book to my beautiful wife, Robyn, who is my greatest blessing and my two wonderful sons, Ricky and Ryan, who are my pride and joy.

ACKNOWLEDGEMENTS

I thank Daniel Aumiller for his marvelous drawing on the cover of this book. He is a tremendous talent and a gift from God. Also, I am grateful for my professors at Fuller Theological Seminary in my doctoral studies: Dr. Bob Logan, Dr. Eddie Gibbs, Dr. Steve Goodwin, and Dr. Kurt Fredrickson. They were a tremendous source of guidance and wisdom in my adventure with Jesus. I especially thank Dr. Tom Parker from the Fuller Theological extension in Phoenix, Arizona, who has been a great friend and source of encouragement for almost twenty years. Furthermore, I am grateful for my mentors Reverend Gale Schmidt and Reverend Bud Eskritt. They sustained me and guided me through some of the toughest years of my pastoral ministry. I thank God for my editors, Judy Pederson and Kristie Savage, whose patience and skills made this book possible. I am eternally grateful to God for my brothers and sister in Christ: Jim Widney, Kelly Preiss, Mike Gardner, Dr. Dennis Parker, Cathy Gardner, and Bridget Aumiller, whom the Lord used to transform my life and the life of Amazing Grace. I have been blessed to work with three very skilled, caring, and professional Chaplains: Chaplain James Holder, Chaplain Kathryn Snell, and Chaplain Debbie Herrera. They made this book possible. I thank Sheriff Arpaio and his detention officers who faithfully and professionally enable us to bring the good news of Jesus into the Maricopa County jails. I praise our Lord for my Amazing Grace church family and leadership who have been a constant support in this effort to love all people to Christ. As always, I thank God for my beautiful wife Robyn who encouraged, motivated, and at times, harassed me to pursue this work. She is "Da Bomb!" Most importantly I give praise to Jesus Christ! This is really all His work.

PREFACE

Twenty four years ago, if someone would have told me I would be writing a Christian book at that time, I would have asked them, "What have you been smoking?" For twenty four years ago, I was, as Hank Williams Jr. would say, "whiskey bent and hell bound". I was a functional alcoholic with a beautiful wife, two great kids, a great job, a new home, and two new cars in the driveway.

Then an amazing thing happened. One night after returning home from a family party, after pounding down a twelve pack of beer, I lay next to my sleeping wife and began to cry. I was tired of the emptiness brought on from the booze. I was tired of my numbing existence. As I wept I prayed, "Jesus, if you are there, then take my life because I don't want it." *Little did I know how that simple prayer of little faith would change my life!* The next day I quit drinking and at the urging of my pastor, I started to read the Bible. In the scriptures I came to know Jesus and my life was changed forever. I started to live the ever-changing adventure of Jesus.

My priorities in life were changed and the most important thing in life for me was to introduce people to Jesus. *Although our eternal destination was important, I wanted people to know Jesus here and now in order to experience real life in the present.* This led to Fuller Theological Seminary, to Pacific Lutheran Theological Seminary, and to ordination in the Evangelical Lutheran Church in America (ELCA). The adventure of Jesus led me into urban ministry and Latino ministry. Yes, Jesus taught me a new language, Spanish.

Mind you I never liked languages and studied four years of French (?) in high school.

All I ever wanted was a call to a nice little church in the suburbs. A suburban church that has maybe one hundred and fifty members to two hundred members who all speak English, a sanctuary and classrooms that were paid for, one or two services on Sunday, and an opportunity to reach people for Jesus in a *civilized arena*. However, the Lord Jesus had different plans in mind. For the thirteen years in which I have served as a pastor, I have served in the city, in a multicultural setting, in churches where monies for mission are scarce, where multiple and varied worship services are necessary, and generally reaching people for Jesus whom other churches might not want. These are the poor, with little or no education, with addictions and untreated family problems, illegal aliens, the divorced, the incarcerated, single parent families, unmarried cohabitating couples with children, and the mentally challenged. This book shares my journey as a pastor and child of God from the secure world of tending the flock with varied programs within the walls of the church, to the mission field within the Maricopa County jails. During this journey the Lord led me to develop a strategy for reaching those incarcerated in the local county jail.

Jesus led me into the toughest jail complex in America to plant jail churches. *The purpose of this book is to share my adventure in Christ and to encourage others to follow Jesus wherever He may lead you.* Hopefully, Jesus will inspire the reader to move into jail or prison ministry in which case this book can act as a resource in the planting of additional jail or prison churches. My prayer for the reader is to *"GO"* and *"FOLLOW"* Jesus wherever He leads you. After all, this book and our lives are really all about Him who lives in us and through us.

TABLE OF CONTENTS

INTRODUCTION

THE JOURNEY INTO JAIL CHURCH PLANTING

By January of 2006, I was simply trying to catch my breath. I was a solo pastor at Amazing Grace Christian Church (hereafter, Amazing Grace), which provided two English worship services and one Spanish worship service. The church had recently gone through an extensive reinvention including leaving the Evangelical Lutheran Church in America (ELCA) in order to partner with Lutheran Congregations in Mission for Christ (LCMC). At this time, Jim Widney, a friend from the Community of Joy Lutheran church, approached me about starting a jail ministry. Jim is a big man and a retired truck driver who has been transformed dramatically by the love of Christ. He admits to having one of the foulest mouths around until Jesus touched him and healed him. Now Jim wants to use this same mouth to love people to Christ. I agreed to help Widney get two jail services started at Lower Buckeye jail. This included training and coaching. We felt very strongly that this was a leading of the Holy Spirit. We decided to take immediate action and to respond to this move of the Spirit. It was not a time for timidity but rather a time for leadership. In contrast, there are too many pastors and church leaders who hesitate when the Spirit calls. When equipped by the Spirit, we have nothing to fear! William Easum and Thomas G. Bandy, in their book, *Growing Spiritual Redwoods*, declare:

In this time of radical change and upheaval, the church desperately needs leaders who are not afraid to lead. Church leaders are called to lead. . . .The general public feels lost, and the Christian public feels powerless. In the midst of such challenge, church leaders are extraordinarily timid. They are terrified they might be perceived to be too aggressive, too disruptive, or too dictatorial. They cling to the myth that the less leadership they offer, the more empowered Christians will be! In fact, the opposite is true. . . .*Where leadership is clearly in evidence, the benefits of empowerment are being achieved and embedded in culture.* Church leaders are called to risk popularity, social status, and pension plans, in order to empower others to envision, birth, and nurture the God-given potential that is within them.[1]

Widney and I launched forward at the Spirit's leading without forming a committee or asking permission. *There are too many times in the local congregation when the movement of the Spirit can be halted in committee.* In my previous call, it had taken us over two years to install a new altar rail. In hindsight this was actually pretty hasty considering how slowly church councils and committees work. The church leadership was informed of the project and there was a sense of excitement. Everyone involved felt this was indeed a movement of the Holy Spirit. The leadership council provided the necessary funding and graciously granted their blessing and support for this new mission. The church council was genuinely enthused and inspired about this mission. It felt good to step out of the box.

The worship services commenced at Lower Buckeye jail, and they were very well received by the inmates. The jail volunteers and I had discovered the difference between rocky and fertile soil as taught in Jesus' parable of the sower in Matthew 13:3-23. The inmates in our jail churches were extremely fertile soil. They were open to receiving the good news of Jesus Christ. The jail worship was averaging thirty inmates at one service and twenty at the second service. Jim Widney and I preached Jesus and many inmates received Him as their Lord. Jim Widney and I also preached that they, the inmates, were the Church and should take what they had experienced back to their pods or cell groups. A pod consists of approximately fifty inmates.[2] They delivered the good news in their pods and an increasing number of inmates began to accept Christ. They began prayer circles and Bible studies in their pods and even celebrated Holy Communion together. One inmate was transferred to the Towers jail, another jail in the Maricopa County jail complex, and he started a Bible study for forty-five inmates. The detention officers noted a difference in the inmates who attended our worship services.

At this point, I attended Robert E. Logan's class at Fuller Seminary in church planting. It was through this class that I realized Amazing Grace had actually planted two churches in the jails. In fact, the inmates were more excited about Christ and more "Christian" than many people who were sitting in the church pews outside the jail complex. *By "Christian," I mean the inmates were more free, honest, authentic, compassionate, sincere, and committed to living in a relationship with Jesus than many people in the local congregations.* After the ten-week follow-up class on the Internet, I realized God was calling our church to continue planting churches in the jail complex. This experience shaped my vision for this book on church planting. This experience has also impacted Widney and the jail pastors (members of Amazing Grace and other churches who pastor the jail churches), as well as the congregation of Amazing Grace. We will never be the same again. The inmates have changed Amazing Grace into a church that seeks to love the outcast and those discarded by society in order to draw them to Christ, due to His love working in the lives of members of the congregation.

In order to reach the lost, those who do not know Jesus, in obedience to Christ's command and in response to Jesus' love, this book will develop a strategy for planting additional jail churches in the Maricopa County jail complex. At the same time the reader can share in our adventure into jail ministry. There is a tremendous need for additional jail churches. Prison Chaplain Richard Shaw, in his book *Chaplains to the Imprisoned*, explains, "A church that is interested in prisoners doesn't have to look."[3] Shaw then quotes Duane Peterson, who observed, "'Every community has at least a jail. . . . It is this nearness that is also part of the shameful neglect by churches for prison ministries. Between fifteen hundred and two thousand jails have no religious services for inmates.'"[4] *The need for jail churches in America in general and Maricopa County, Arizona specifically is apparent.* Amazing Grace is attempting to meet the need for jail churches in the Maricopa County jail complex and provide a model for other churches across America.

This aforementioned strategy will also address connecting these churches with the mother church, Amazing Grace, through developing and maintaining an ongoing relationship with the inmates. Connecting church members and inmates is difficult and at times impossible for many churches. Shaw writes: "The large and wealthy mainline denominations offer bold pronouncements on criminal justice almost yearly at their national meetings. They are on record against the death penalty; most have written detailed statements criticizing incarceration and living conditions in prisons. But that is often where it ends."[5] Amazing Grace will take the next step and embrace the inmates as part of its community.

This book will focus on a strategy to convert the inmates in jail into disciples of Jesus Christ by planting additional churches in the Maricopa County jail complex. The purpose is to impact the lives of inmates at the jail complex with the love of Christ and at the same time establish a loving relationship with the local church in order to continue their lives in the Christian community upon their release. Lennie Spitale, director of prison ministries for Vision in New England, declares:

> The love of Christ is the power and purpose of these new churches. . . .You will find yourself being used as a vessel of Christ's compassion. No matter if you received a specific, unique calling, as I did, or whether you went out of simple obedience and found yourself liking it, this matters little as long as your primary motivation remains the love of Christ. That is what counts. "For Christ's love compels us, because we are convinced that one died for all, and therefore all died. (2 Cor. 5:14)"[6]

Part One will focus on the ministry context and history of Amazing Grace. It will also examine the churches in the Maricopa County jail complex and the unchurched inmates. The challenge with doing mission in the Maricopa County jails is there are many inmates who were previously members of a church but were not disciples of Jesus Christ. Chaplains W. Thomas Beckner and Jeff Park state:

> During one presentation, I stopped my teaching to ask the inmate audience, well over 450 men, a very poignant question, "How many of you came to this prison genuine but backslidden Christians?" My volunteer team and I gasped as we saw well over half of the audience's hands raise in the affirmative. After four decades of ministry and observation of how the Gospel transforms lives, this response was not an indictment of the power of the Gospel, but it was certainly an indictment on how we (perhaps more the Church than prison ministry volunteers) present the Gospel.[7]

Other inmates have never heard the Good News of Jesus Christ. Still others have been de-churched by the community of faith at some time in their lives. In all of these cases, these inmates have never really experienced the life-changing love of Jesus. They need to be converted. As previously mentioned, the inmates at the Maricopa County jail complex are very fertile soil for the transforming love of Christ. They are people who have lost everything and are very open to the Gospel.

Part Two will reflect on the theological foundations for planting additional jail churches, converting inmates, and connecting them with Amazing Grace or another Christian church upon their release. Regarding the need for jail churches, Beckner and Park write:

> Now, however, as the state-funded institutional chaplain is being systematically eliminated, there is a need for a larger base of support for correctional ministry. In order to be effective in the future, chaplaincy will need the broad support of church denominations and local congregations, as citizens

and community leaders who are willing to partner with chaplains in delivering ministry services. The model of chaplaincy for the future will demand that the entire Christian community unite in a combined effort to a crucial societal problem. [8]

The theological concepts of "fertile soil," "the foolish things of God," discipleship, and the enthusiasm of new converts to Christianity will also be explored. These theological considerations are necessary in the planting of jail churches. This part of the book will include a definition of jail church, why we call it a church, how it can be called a church and the absolute necessity of the power of prayer in planting churches.

Part Three will address the strategy of developing prayer cover or prayer intercessors, starting additional jail churches, discerning the call of being a jail pastor, providing life-changing worship opportunities for inmates, connecting these jail churches with the mother church (in this case, Amazing Grace), and involving the membership with the conversion and life change of inmates. This connection is of the utmost importance in maintaining the inmates' faith upon release. Prison Chaplain Henry G. Covert, in his book *Ministry to the Incarcerated*, explains:

> There is nothing more important for released prisoners than aftercare. After all, these individuals seldom have the resources to become stable citizens on their own. They need assistance that begins while they are still incarcerated. In other words, networking prior to release is necessary to prevent inmates from being overwhelmed by the new challenges of freedom, whether they receive support from a local church, a counseling agency, a therapeutic center, a workshop, or a job training program. Many individuals and organizations can assist returning felons but only through community awareness and inmate networking. [9]

This proposed strategy will serve as a model for other churches to follow in order to establish jail churches and provide follow-up for released inmates. I pray that the reader will endeavor to begin their own journey into planting jail churches. This section will also include a means to evaluate life change in the jails and in the mother church. *This book offers a way for the local congregation to reach outside itself in love to those whom society has cast out. In so doing, the congregation is no longer a self-absorbed organization but a mission for Jesus Christ.* As Eddie Gibbs writes, "The day of the local church is over; the day of the mission outpost has come."[10]

PART ONE:

CONTEXT OF AMAZING GRACE CHRISTIAN CHURCH AND THE MARICOPA COUNTY JAILS

CHAPTER 1

MINISTRY CONTEXT OF AMAZING GRACE CHRISTIAN CHURCH

History and Lutheran Roots

My Journey as Pastor

In December of 2002, I was assigned as a part-time interim pastor to Advent Lutheran Church, later to be renamed Amazing Grace Christian Church. Advent Lutheran Church had been started in 1964 by the Lutheran Church in America (LCA, the church body that preceded the Evangelical Lutheran Church in America, or ELCA), in the suburbs of Glendale, Arizona. At the time, this was a predominately white middle-class neighborhood. The church had never blossomed into a large, thriving congregation. In fact, the weekly worship attendance topped at approximately 135 people. They never really sought the lost. Their Lutheran heritage and theology unconsciously stopped them from seeking the lost. In Luther's Small Catechism, Martin Luther writes:

> I believe that by my own reason or strength I cannot believe in Jesus Christ, my Lord, or come to Him. But the Holy Spirit has called me through the Gospel, enlightened me

with His gifts, and sanctified and preserved me in the true faith, just as He calls, gathers, enlightens, and sanctifies the whole Christian church on earth and preserves it in union with Jesus Christ in the one true faith.[1]

Generally, the Lutheran churches in America have interpreted this to mean *evangelism was the sole responsibility of the Holy Spirit.* All that is required of the Church is to build a structure and let the Holy Spirit fill it with people. Advent Lutheran Church thought it was fulfilling the Great Commission. However, in reality, Advent Lutheran Church was considered a dying church for the last twenty years by the denominational hierarchy of the ELCA as well as by the surrounding churches. In fact, the former bishop told the church council at a council meeting in the early 1990s, "The church should put out a sign that said *Mission Was Accomplished,* and close the church property."

I arrived after the church had been served for ten years by another part-time pastor, who was basically serving as a chaplain while the church was breathing its last breaths. The week before my arrival, there were only twenty-three people at worship. During the summer, worship attendance fell to six or eight people. The church council had decided to spend its savings in one last attempt to call a pastor and save Advent Lutheran.

It was shocking to discover that in the previous ten years there had not been one adult Bible study offered. The council president and vice president stated that the church needed to focus on increasing worship numbers and revenue. *I told them they needed to focus on Jesus and bringing people to Jesus and then the numbers and revenue would fall into place.* They decided to call me to be their permanent pastor. I asked them to wait and see what God had in mind. I was not in the right frame of mind to accept a call having just resigned from my previous call over adverse circumstances. The infighting and stress had taken its toll on me. Furthermore, a church worshipping six people is a questionable call. Do they need a chaplain or a pastor? In the meantime, they sent to the bishop's office an interim contract stating that the congregation would like to consider calling me, the interim pastor, permanently. This is against ELCA policy but, surprisingly, the bishop approved it.

I knew that Advent Lutheran Church needed to change drastically in order to survive and as an interim pastor, I had the freedom to boldly introduce change. After all, as an interim pastor, I would only be there for a limited time and I felt I had nothing to lose. At this time I was blessed to be mentored by Pastor Bud Eskritt in the duties of an interim. Bud was a semi-retired pastor who served the synod in the most difficult interim calls possible. He served in one toxic situation after another and maintained his health and sanity. I was astonished at Bud's intestinal fortitude. Ironically, the bishop recommended this mentoring relationship. Therefore with Pastor Bud's approval, *I recommended they rename the church, change the worship format, formulate a mission statement, and adopt a new constitution that was permission-giving and not restrictive to the mission of Jesus Christ.* To my amazement, the church supported all of the changes. The membership voted to change the name to Amazing Grace Christian Church (hereafter, Amazing Grace) because most people did not know what the terms "Advent" or "Lutheran" meant. There was some initial fallout as four family units of the original twenty-three worshippers left the church. When people leave their local congregation, it is always a painful experience. The leadership of the church still supported me in regard to the many new changes. As an interim pastor, this support was vital. In the end, the departure of these members did not discourage me. In fact, the church leadership and I later saw it as a "blessed reduction," to quote John Wesley.

The church began growing numerically and spiritually. We added another worship opportunity. The new worship service, although blended, was much more contemporary. I asked the Lord for a sign that this was where He wanted me to serve. I asked the Lord to have one hundred people worship by Easter Sunday. Easter Sunday arrived and 146 people were at worship. God is so very faithful! I excitedly informed the bishop of the progress the church was making and I found myself called into the bishop's office the following day. I was shocked to find the bishop was *reprimanding me* for exceeding the boundaries of an interim pastor. I felt that whether

I was called as the pastor or someone else, it would be better to have a church with people in it as opposed to an empty building. The bishop clearly told me to stop all evangelistic activity and to do nothing but preach on Sundays for the next six months as I awaited a call to serve as another church's permanent pastor. After leaving the bishop's office, I prayerfully decided there was no way I could sit back and let this church die. I believe the Lord has given me the gift of evangelism and to not use this gift would be a sin. Leonard Sweet states, "What is the worst thing that can happen to me? Not to lose my life. But to not be where Jesus is."[2] Jesus would not choose to have a church close its doors especially after the number of people who worshipped on Easter Sunday. As the interim pastor, I decided to follow Jesus. I had no idea how this decision would change my life and the life of Amazing Grace. I was affirmed of my decision in Bob Logan's class at Fuller. *During class Bob warned us that there would be times in our ministry when we would have to choose to follow Jesus or our church hierarchy. He firmly stated to follow Jesus. He went on to say that this choice held eternal consequences.* I believe Dr. Logan's words were God breathed.

I contacted the council president and said I would be taking a risk for Amazing Grace and that I would need his promise of support. I did not share any part of the discussion in the bishop's office with the president. The council president promised his support without asking any questions. We had developed quite a bond of trust over the past five months.

The church adopted a new mission statement, which is to "love all people to Christ by becoming Jesus' followers and celebrating the ever-changing adventure of Jesus." This is an adaptation of my personal mission statement. As Amazing Grace embraced this mission statement, the worship numbers and ministries began to increase. In fact, we were worshipping between 60 and 100 people at Amazing Grace. In June of 2003, Amazing Grace decided to call me as their permanent, full-time pastor. When the congregational leadership notified the bishop, I was called back into the bishop's office. This time I was forced to sign a six-page written reprimand or the bishop would not sign my letter of call to Amazing Grace. The reprimand quoted the ELCA's constitution but never once quoted

Scripture or the Lutheran Confessions. *The reprimand was a lie but I reluctantly signed it.* In addition, the bishop met privately with the church council for a consultation without my presence. I discovered later that consultation consisted of the bishop, verbally attacking not only me but also my wife. In spite of the reprimand, the church unanimously voted to call me and I was installed as the full-time pastor in August 2003.

Amazing Grace's Journey out of the denomination

The church continued to grow and Amazing Grace even paid over three thousand dollars benevolence to the ELCA. The congregational leaders and I desired to have a new beginning with the church hierarchy. As Amazing Grace grew, it received some Latino members into the fellowship. The church's neighborhood is now 42 percent Latino, so this came as no surprise. One of the Latino members recommended they start a free English as a Second Language (ESL) course, with nursery provided free of charge. Amazing Grace responded positively to her request and discovered they had to limit their first ESL class to forty-five students with twenty children in the nursery. In 2004, at the request of the teacher and students of the ESL course, the church decided to start a Spanish worship service in spite of my very limited Spanish language skills. The church leadership informed the bishop's office of the new mission opportunity. The congregational leadership and I were told not to start a Latino ministry. *It seems Amazing Grace's Latino ministry did not fit into the denomination's multicultural mission strategy. Part of the problem for the bishop's office was that I was Caucasian. The hierarchy wanted Latinos doing Latino ministry.* Mike Regele and Mark Schultz in their book *Death of the Church* describe the situation with the bishop very well when they state:

> One of the greatest challenges facing the church in America today is, Will we let real leaders lead? Or, will we drive them out of our systems? Under the rubric of accountability, too many visionary leaders are driven out of a denominational tradition by denominational gatekeepers. Gatekeepers do not drive them away out of true moral accountability to

the Gospel. They drive them out for fear of true leadership! People will follow true leaders. In too many cases this is exactly what the gatekeepers fear.[3]

The church began the Spanish worship service despite the bishop's lack of approval and once again, the Lord blessed the ministry and provided people and funding. Presently, the denomination has halted the planting of new Latino missions in Arizona. At this time, I was enrolled in a Doctor of Ministry course at Fuller Theological Seminary titled "Turn-Around Churches."[4] Taught by Steve Goodwin, the class focused on paradigm shifts and church reformation. During this time I began to see that the culture had changed and the greater Church was going through an upheaval. The bishop and Amazing Grace were part of a much larger transformation taking place in the United States. The two were being torn apart by a movement much larger than the immediate situation.

By now, the people at Amazing Grace were upset with the continual interference and lack of support by the denominational office. Then the bishop informed all the churches that a six-week study on homosexuality was *mandated* by the denomination. Amazing Grace participated in this mandated study and discovered that the written material was biased in favor of the homosexual lifestyle. Furthermore, in the study, Scriptural authority was dismissed and a revisionist interpretation of Scripture employed. *It really is not a revisionist interpretation; it is false teaching.*

Amazing Grace's beliefs were confirmed and crystallized with the completion of the homosexuality study. The congregation felt the denomination had discarded the authority of Scripture and placed it on par with human experience and scientific hypothesis. It also appeared that the hierarchy wanted to control outreach and mission in the local congregations. *This is contrary to Scripture and the Lutheran Confessions. It is false teaching.* Furthermore, it was contrary to at least three of the church's core values: "evangelism/ all inclusive," "the authority of Scripture," and "the freedom to be who we are in Christ." It also blatantly contradicted and restricted the church's mission and vision statements (see Appendix A). The mission statement includes "loving all people to Christ," and the vision statement includes "reaching out in love to all people." The words "all people" refer to Latinos as well as Caucasians. *This local congregation discovered the mainline denomination was not Christian mainline but secular culture mainline.* Amazing Grace was in agreement with Paul G. Hiebert, who declares: "The greatest danger is that we accept our social organization and our culture without being aware of it and thereby become its captive. All human systems need to be brought under the lordship of Christ and his kingdom."[5] Amazing Grace did not want to be captive to the denomination, nor to the postmodern culture.

As a group, the local congregation asked, "What are we doing in this very secular institutional church?" The members realized that they were miles apart from the denomination's mission and theology. Rodney Clapp, in his book *A Peculiar People: The Church as Culture in a Post-Christian Society*, states:

> The only churches that grow today are those that do not, in fact, understand the issues, and can therefore traffic in certainty (Jesus Christ). They represent both the fundamentalist Protestant groups and rigidly controlled conservative Catholic traditions. The churches that do attempt to interact with the emerging world are for the most part liberal Protestant mainline churches that shrink every day in membership and the silent liberal Catholic minority that attracts very few adherents. Both are, almost by definition, fuzzy, imprecise and relatively unappealing. They might claim to be honest, but for the most part they have no real message.[6]

Amazing Grace contacted Lutheran Congregations in Mission for Christ (hereafter LCMC), a voluntary association of Lutheran churches that believes the local congregation should be more autonomous. *LCMC is also orthodox in its theology and biblically based. LCMC still has a message. LCMC still believes there is no other source that is on par with Scripture.* Amazing Grace joined LCMC in the spring of 2004.

In July 2004, I resigned from the denomination's clergy roster and joined the LCMC clergy roster. In response, I received a three-page "hate" letter from the bishop. I was shocked and hurt by the viciousness of the letter. I have found much comfort in Luther's words: "It is by living . . . no rather, by dying and being damned that a theologian is made, not by understanding, reading, or speculating."[7] *Once again, the denominational constitution was quoted but neither the Scriptures nor Lutheran Confessions were ever mentioned nor referenced in this letter.* I shared the bishop's letter with the congregational council. They were angered by the hateful language and lies expressed by an acting bishop.

Later, I discovered from my LCMC colleagues that such ruthless behavior by bishops involved in church conflict is not unusual. The following story exhibits the bishops' *gatekeeper mentality.* This is a true story described by Rev. Dr. Norman David of Massachusetts (names have been changed for the benefit of all):

Subject: Re: Bishop Brown & St. Luke's

Dear Steve:

The president of Christ Lutheran, Belmont, whose name is Ilmars, is from Latvia and his family had to flee Nazi oppression in the 1930s and came to America. He uses the term "blackshirts" to refer to representatives of ELCA New England Bishop Smith who dress up in their most formidable looking black clergy suits with black shirts and white collars and on a warm afternoon in spring (May 10, 2002) descend on little ol' Christ Lutheran play yard to confront Kelly, a non-church-member who is a teacher in our Nursery School, as she plays with the children awaiting their parents to pick them up at 2 p.m.

This formidable group of five were headed by two Assistants to the Bishop, Rev. Rogers and Rev. Griffin, and three members of the Synod Council, Rev. Pax, and two others, all acting on clandestine orders from Bishop Smith to get the teacher's key to the church and hand her and the parents coming to pick up the children letters from Bishop Smith declaring she is taking over operations of the congregation, suspending the Pastor and his wife [who is a trustee of the church], and forbidding them to enter church property. It advises the parents to seek another school for their children because she cannot guarantee that Christ Lutheran of Belmont will be around for much longer.

Kelly reluctantly produced her key, which they swiped from her hand and turned over to a locksmith who began changing the locks on the church building.

This group of "Blackshirts" then went through the church building looking for church records they could confiscate to the Synod office. They broke down one door that was locked. They had the windows nailed shut, interdicted the phone service to have all calls to the church number forwarded to the Bishop's office, and then set up a little waiting party for Yours Truly.

All this was being done without any consultation with or knowledge by any member or participant in the Christ Lutheran congregation, which owns the property and always has, pays its own bills and always has, calls its own minister and operates its own programs and ministries apart from any Bishop involvement, has never had any debt to Synod and has ceded no authority to Synod or Bishop to act in this manner. It was purely a case of Bishop Smith trying to force the "Bishop-rules" model on the local congregation without the congregation's invitation or permission.

Out-ra-ge-ous!!

While all this is going on, the president of Christ Lutheran and I were sitting in the office of Rev. Fred… Fred, whom I used to consider a colleague and friend, had been persuaded by Bishop Smith into hosting a meeting between her and me and Ilmars in Fred's presence at Lutheran Church of the Cross, some five miles away, where he is pastor. According to a carefully worked out agreement between Bishop Smith and me, this meeting was to be a time for open and honest dialogue between her and me and our congregational president about the future of Christ Lutheran. Smith wanted it closed because she thought it too small to be viable (and she had ideas about what to do with the assets!). Ilmars and I represented the congregation's majority opinion that there was potential in other directions for the church that we were ready to tap, and, in any event, did not want to be rushed into closure as Smith had tried to do with another congregation in downtown Boston two years prior.

But it was all a setup! Smith had no intention of dialoguing; her letters were printed before the meeting began and she had her black-shirt takeover party dispatched even as we poured out our hearts to her in Fred's office. She used it as a ruse to tie us up for two hours.

She didn't speak much and, after letting Ilmars and I speak for some length, produced a letter informing us that I was suspended as Pastor, that operation of the congregation was being taken over by her, and that I and my wife were forbidden to enter the church property unless we had her written permission! I learned some time later that Fred was apprised of this plan before the meeting began and although he was uncomfortable with it and told Bp. Smith that this was not a good idea, he went along with it like a loyal lap dog.

Ilmars and I left that meeting scratching our heads as to what Smith met about "taking over" CLC. She'd have to get the okay from Congregational Meeting, which she hadn't sought yet. When we turned the corner and approached the church, our jaws dropped to see the "blackshirts" standing in the open doorway of the building! They had the gall to force their way in and bash open doors, just like '39 in Germany!

After it was determined by several hurried phone calls from my house next door that no one knew anything about what was going on, and after the Director of the Nursery School and three of the staff, who responded to Kelly's call, told us in tears how the black-shirts had rudely told them to stay out of the way and not inter-fere, for The Bishop was now in control of the church, we called the cops. The police responded with a patrol car and two officers. We told them that unauthorized persons were trespassing on church grounds and that they should be escorted off the premises. With a call to headquarters, they were informed that the Chief of Police, after being informed by Bishop Smith some days earlier that she would be taking this action and it was entirely within the right of the Bishop to do so, gave his word that the police would not interfere, except to keep the peace. Outraged that the local police in Belmont, among whom my wife and I have lived and been civic leaders for over 25 years (she a three-term elected official on the Belmont Board of Health) would give this permission to a stranger—Bishop Smith—without checking out her claim with the pastor or president of Christ Lutheran Church—a fixture in the community since 1937, we were told to work it out with our lawyer.

We did. The law was on our side. The congregation was advised by counsel to retake possession of the property and reassert its right of ownership. The next morning I found an open window which the locksmith had failed to nail shut (the only one, and I found it on the first try and didn't discover that they had nailed the windows until several days later). We called in our own locksmith to change the locks again for us, and had a nice welcoming party for two of the blackshirts when they came the next Sunday to conduct the morning service on behalf of the Bishop. Now we are an independent congregation, having terminated membership in the ELCA in November 2002. However, we look to apply for membership in the LCMC later this year...

I include this story to demonstrate the outrageous and ruthless behavior of the denomination. The denominational hierarchy is more concerned about preserving the institution than in shepherding the flock. The Amazing Grace council and I felt affirmed in our actions after we read Dr. David's letter. *The new reformation is bigger than just us!* I have included this letter not just to give additional background regarding our departure from the denomination but to encourage others who may be experiencing a similar decision or persecution. Please take heart and continue to follow Jesus. Please remember John's words, "You, dear children, are from God and have overcome them, because *the one who is in you is greater than the one who is in the world. 5They* are from the world and therefore speak from the viewpoint of the world, and the world listens to them."(1John 4: 4-5)

In February 2005, the denomination removed Amazing Grace from the denominational congregational roster, giving the congregation freedom and full rights to the church property. The Lord has continued to bless Amazing Grace numerically, financially, and spiritually as the church strives to love all people to Christ. The freedom the church has experienced since the denominational break has been a tremendous blessing. *However, there is a price that has been paid in departing the denomination. The local church lost many sister congregations and I have lost many beloved colleagues. Leaving the denomination was a very heartrending process.* The security and backup of a multimillion-dollar institution is now gone. Amazing Grace's security and backup is now rightfully found solely in the person of Jesus Christ.

This reformation was not planned but evolved over time. In fact, as Lyle Schaller claims in his book, *The New Reformation: Tomorrow Arrived Today*, the Christian Church is truly in the midst of another great reformation. Like Schaller, "I was focusing on the renewal of the old and failed to see a new reformation in American Christianity already was well underway."[8] I wonder to what extent the congregation consciously made choices or was simply swept along by the greater wave of reformation sweeping through the American Church. The reformation picked up momentum at Amazing Grace from the actions and reactions of the bishop and the denomination. Amazing Grace never had any intention of leaving its denomination but felt it was forced to take a stand. Our denomination was not unlike many mainline Protestant churches, which Regele and Schultz contend have "highlighted for us the dangers of completely leveling the playing field of ideas—making it equally valid and valuable. This is simply not true, and out of faithfulness to the Gospel and people who need to hear the Word of God through the confusion, we must be willing to say, 'It is this, not that.'"[9] The members of Amazing Grace have taken a stand regarding God's Word. Amazing Grace has said regarding the truth of God's Word, "It is this, and not that." Amazing Grace feels it took this stand for Jesus and that He is its center. Although a painful experience, the local church has no regrets in its decision and believes it is truly following Jesus Christ and not men.

Amazing Grace's Entry into Jail Ministry

As mentioned in the introduction, in 2006 I had a conversation with a good friend, Jim Widney. Widney is a bear of a man with a burning passion in his heart for Jesus Christ. As we talked, Widney shared with me his heartfelt desire to minister in the Maricopa County jails. I responded that I too had felt the Lord leading me into jail ministry through my doctoral studies at Fuller Seminary with Dr. Bob Logan and my participation in a Spanish jail service with a bilingual pastor. At this serendipitous and Spirit-led meeting, we decided to pursue the mission of planting a church in the Maricopa County jail complex. I presented the project to the Amazing Grace church council, and they welcomed the plan and provided financing. Amazing Grace is a church whose mission is to love all people to Christ; hence, it decided to take the risk and provide the needed resources.

The first two jail churches were planted in the Lower Buckeye jail, a men's facility. In 2007, two additional jail churches were added in the Estrella jail, a facility for women. Unfortunately at this time, Widney discontinued serving one jail church at Lower Buckeye because it was physically too demanding on him. The Lord has provided jail pastors to lead these additional jail churches and the rewards to the local churches involved have been phenomenal.

The spiritual growth of the members of Amazing Grace as a result of its jail churches is rapidly increasing. This growth was stimulated by the taking of personal prayer requests from inmates to the congregation and the inmates praying for Amazing Grace. As released inmates become members of the church, the members of the local church have matured even more in their faith. As a result of the jail churches, the members of Amazing Grace grew in their worship attendance, Bible study attendance, prayer life, and stewardship. When they heard the testimonies of the released inmates who attend the church, they grew in their openness and willingness to tell their own stories and to share prayer requests. *What began as a mission to love the inmates to Christ completely reversed. The local church found itself being transformed by the love of Christ in the inmates.* The members of Amazing Grace began by giving away both financial and people resources, which is a risk for an urban church, but they discovered the Lord abundantly blessing them. I have come to believe the key to growth in the local church comes from simply giving it all away. Missionary Raymond Rosales, in his book, *It's about Mission! Ventures and Views of a Pilgrim in Hispanic Ministry*, describes the experience of Amazing Grace over the past few years succinctly. He declares:

God calls us not to go here and there. The heart of His call is to follow Jesus, and ultimately become fishers of men. The disciples all threw in their lots with the Lord after a definite decision. The example was given of Moses; he threw himself in with the lot of the Israelites, even though they were slaves, and Egypt offered him wealth, education, and honor. When we answer the call of God, instead of our being fishers of men, God says that He has some "making" to do in us.

The principle tenet in the beginning is the abandonment to leadership of God. The great men of the Bible (e.g., Abraham, Elisha) in almost every case took a drastic step to break with everything in order to follow God.

The making of disciples seems to be a test on God's claim on them. After years of aimless following, they did not have the foggiest idea of any program. In God's time, God's orders crystallized for them personally. God may lead us into strange places and through much aimless following to test His claim on us.[10]

This brief and recent history of Amazing Grace helps define the context of the mother church in this book. It is evident that Amazing Grace is united and no stranger to change or risk. These are two characteristics that will benefit the congregation in planting additional jail churches.

Reinvention and Openness to Change as Derived from Amazing Grace's Core Values and Mission Statements

Over the past six years Amazing Grace Christian Church has done some in-depth self-examination and soul-searching. The church completed two Natural Church Development (NCD) surveys, developed by Christian Schwarz.[11] In the NCD surveys, a church defines and focuses on improving one of the eight key factors for church growth and development. The factor to be focused on is one in need of the greatest improvement. It is called "the minimum factor." In improving this minimum factor, the other seven factors also naturally improve. This process leads to church health which is necessary in planting jail churches.

Amazing Grace also adapted and embraced my personal mission statement: "To love all people to Christ, to become his disciples, and to enjoy the ever-changing adventure of Jesus." The church's mission statement is: *To love all people to Christ by becoming Jesus' followers and by enjoying the ever-changing adventure of Jesus.* Later, as a result of my attending Goodwin's "Turn-Around Churches" class, Amazing Grace developed core values and created and adopted a vision statement. I used processes and techniques learned in Goodwin's class to lead the church in these endeavors. The church's core values are: Christ alone (John 14:6), love (Matt. 22:37-38), community (John 13:34-35), evangelism/all-inclusiveness (Matt. 28:18-20), prayer (Matt. 21:22), discipleship (Matt. 16:24), authority of Scripture (2 Tim. 3:16-17), freedom to be who we are in Christ (John 8:36), and hope (Rom. 15:13). The core value of hope was added in January 2008 at the recommendation of the inmates of a jail church. The core value that surfaced first and foremost in the surveys for the church's core values was love.

As stated above, the mission of Amazing Grace is to "love all people to Christ by becoming Jesus' followers and celebrating the ever-changing adventure of Jesus." This mission statement guides Amazing Grace in all its ministries. In June of 2003, during one of the many conflicts with the denominational hierarchy, the council president pulled me into the sanctuary and showed me a large banner with the mission statement on it. *He said, "Pastor, that (mission statement) has made all the difference here. That is what we are about. Forget the Synod office."*[12] After adopting the mission statement, the church began understanding its purpose and identity and the momentum accelerated in the church. Amazing Grace was now, more than ever, a God-movement. Continuing today, every council decision is first weighed against whether it aligns with the mission statement. If it does not, the idea is voted down.

A church's vision statement, according to Peter M. Senge, "is a picture of the future you seek to create. . . . [A] statement of our vision shows where we want to go, and what we will be like when we get there."[13] The vision for Amazing Grace is: "We will be a growing and changing community in Christ, reaching out in love to all people, and free to risk all in serving Christ."

Through this experience of reinvention and reformation, Amazing Grace has grown into a changing and risk-taking congregation that is focused on following Jesus. The congregation is very open to change and experimentation if it coincides with the mission statement. The adventure into the jails was literally a match made in heaven. Amazing Grace is a congregation of risk-takers. Chuck Smith, Jr., in his book, *The End of the World . . . As We Know It*, emphasizes:

> The church needs men and women who are not afraid of leaving the security of the past, people who will hoist their mainsail and head into uncharted waters of the future, people who believe God is always on the horizon. The church needs adventurers who ask nothing for the journey besides the North Star of Scripture to guide them, the wind of the Spirit to propel them, and an occasional spray in their face to refresh them. And with this mettle, God can build a church that will rock the postmodern world.[14]

Amazing Grace consists largely of adventurers. Amazing Grace may not be "rocking the world" but it is definitely rocking some lives in the Maricopa County jail complex.

Demographics of the Local Community

Amazing Grace is located in Glendale, Arizona. According to the city of Glendale's full demographic profile as found on its web site, the church resides in the "city geographical area B." Within this neighborhood, the median age is 30.7 years of age. In addition, 32.8 percent are age nineteen or younger.[15] This means there are many young adults and young families in the neighborhood. *It was also projected that by 2007 (the census was taken in 2000), the neighborhood would be 42.5 percent Latino.*[16] *Overall, the report affirmed Amazing Grace's move into Latino ministry and ESL.* The church is in a multicultural setting and the need for a Latino ministry and ESL was obvious. In addition, the average household income for the neighborhood is $45,063 and the average cost of a home is under $99,999. Only 31 percent of the population has graduated from high school.[17]

The neighborhood would be categorized as lower-middle class. These findings are very significant in regard to starting jail churches. *The occupants of this neighborhood do not have a high level of education and are more likely to be incarcerated.* Chaplain Bob Schwarz, author of *You Came unto Me: A Training Manual for Jail and Prison Ministry*, confirms, "Often the educational level of inmates is low."[18] At the same time these people lack the extra income to pay for a defense attorney when they or a family member encounter legal problems or incarceration. Hence, they are more likely to be convicted of a crime. Maricopa County Sheriff Joe Arpaio explains:

On the other side of prison bars, poor defendants frequently receive inadequate representation, while the rich can stall and frustrate the system, eventually winning simply by outspending and outlasting the prosecution. In certain high profile cases, we have seen news media actually become a force in pushing the decision in one direction or another.[19]

Without funds to pay for a private attorney or pay a bond, the family procures the services of a public defender. Chaplain Henry G. Covert, in his book, *Ministry to the Incarcerated*, states:

Using a public defender may eliminate financial concerns, but other problems still exist. These lawyers carry large case-loads and little time for court preparation. Many defendants do not see their public defender until the week of trial, which undoubtedly impairs their defense. When we consider the magnitude of some cases and the potential prison sentence involved, such behavior indicates that the legal system has major flaws. A large number of public defenders are inexperienced in criminal cases. In fact, some of them are recent law school graduates. These individuals acquire their positions to gain knowledge of the legal system and make professional contacts. While this may benefit the attorney, it can spell disaster for the defendant. Moreover, public defenders and district attorneys sometimes make agreements to ease the burden of going to trial at the expense of the defendant.[20]

Ultimately, when people living in the neighborhood surrounding Amazing Grace encounter legal trouble, they end up in one of the county jails. Generally, they remain there until a plea bargain is reached. One former female inmate, now a member at Amazing Grace, was incarcerated in the Estrella jail for twenty-two months until she signed a plea. The system simply wore down her resolve.

Hence, according to the full demographic profile, for Amazing Grace to plant jail churches is very much a means of reaching families in the immediate neighborhood at the same time. The neighborhood understands the workings of the legal and jail system, and has experienced them firsthand in many cases. Furthermore, it appeared from the demographic data that it would be favorable to commence a Spanish jail church.

Makeup of Congregants and their Perception of Jail Ministry

The members of Amazing Grace generally fit the demographic profile of the neighborhood. However, many of the members are new believers. The church has averaged six adult baptisms per year during the last three years.[21] In addition, there are many renewed believers who previously were de-churched. Regele and Schultz describe these members:

> Whether they attended or were active in their faith is not the issue. *The issue is simple: We lost them.* Or better, they have rejected the message of the church as they have understood and perceived it. Quite frankly, it does little good to provide ourselves with explanations and justifications. Certainly, some of them are valid. But the fact remains, these people have become completely and thoroughly disenchanted with any form of religious faith. . . . *We lost them through hurting them.*[22]

At some time in the past, most of the members of Amazing Grace have encountered problems with a local church. The church has marginalized, ignored, or attacked these individuals. Regele and Schultz also write,

> The common thread almost all these new members have is they have all been mistreated or discarded from the church previously. They are de-churched. I believe they "left the institutional church for two reasons. One, it was not what it proclaimed to be. Two, it was merciless in its dealings. It was not God, nor the gospel that drove them away. It was us!"[23]

At Amazing Grace these previously de-churched people are the growing majority. Many of these de-churched are former inmates and inmates' families who are extremely enthusiastic about their faith and their new church home. *The common thread is the love of Christ they have received through this community of faith. Unfortunately, this is usually the first church in which they have been loved unconditionally.*

Having experienced Christ's love, these new and renewed believers are very open to all people. There is a wonderful desire to pass this newfound love on to others. It does not matter if the people are recently released or incarcerated; many of these formerly de-churched members have been there. They know what it means to be ignored or disdained. The membership of Amazing Grace is clear in its mission and the church simply wants Jesus to have his way in its life. John Fischer, in his book, *12 Steps for the Recovering Pharisee (Like Me)*, describes this attitude:

> In the same way, we can be religious and do all sorts of things for God, but if these are not done in humble dependence on Christ, they will amount to nothing. We need to relinquish control over "what we do for God," and trust wholly in what God does in and through us as we live and walk by faith. . . . If you've been given mercy, you don't care who else gets it.

Give it to the whole world for all you care; you are thankful that you got it. [24]

The members of Amazing Grace are thankful that they have received the grace of God and are eager to pass it on, even if this means going into the Maricopa County jail complex. The unique makeup of this congregation is tailored by God to plant jail churches. This does not mean other churches are incapable of planting jail churches; any *healthy* congregation can plant a jail church.

The Core of Disciples and their Perception of Jail Ministry

The core group of disciples at Amazing Grace has grown in recent years due to Cursillo,[25] the Alpha Program,[26] and the established jail churches. Approximately 30 percent of the church is made up of disciples.[27] The church council is drawn from this core of disciples. They are justly and duly placed in leadership positions. Disciples are people who are fully committed to Jesus and willing to sacrifice in order to have God's kingdom come. They do not only worship one hour a week; they faithfully give of their time, talent, and treasure to support the mission of the local church. They are in love with Jesus and his Word and continually strive to grow in their faith. Fischer explains,

> Old is not a part of the vocabulary of faith. Learning, growing, yearning for more, seeing things from other perspectives—this is how we stay young in the faith. The definition of a disciple is a learner, and there is no evidence that the disciples ever ceased being disciples. Once a learner, always a learner. Read the New Testament and substitute "learners" for "disciples" and you might more readily find yourself among them. These were not spiritual giants; like us they were people in process.[28]

These learners or people in progress are an integral part of the leadership at Amazing Grace and many have been through the numerous changes of the past six years. They strive to grow in Christ through study of the Word, prayer, worship, and service. They have embraced the mission statement in its entirety including the third part, which states, "by enjoying the ever-changing adventure of Jesus." They are not afraid to risk for Jesus and are very open to the Spirit's leading. Erwin McManus describes disciples, including those at Amazing Grace, as "children of the wind." In his book, *An Unstoppable Force*, McManus explains:

> The world looks different when you understand yourself to be a child of the wind. You realize, when your sail is up, God's wind blows you to places you never imagined, at just the right moment for someone else. The apostolic ethos is an environment in which all of God's people are guided by the wind. If all are not apostles, at least all are together on the apostolic mission.[29]

The disciples of Amazing Grace have been blown by the wind of the Spirit into Latino ministry, ESL, LCMC and jail ministry. These children of the wind are united in the ever-changing adventure of Jesus.

Furthermore, these disciples maintain the unity and focus in the church. In regard to jail church planting, they see it as a mission commanded by Christ and led by the Holy Spirit. They partake in the leadership and do not simply obey the orders of the pastor. The leadership at Amazing Grace has developed a means of communal discernment or decision making, a collaborative effort which will be discussed in some depth in Chapter 5 of this book pertaining to jail pastors. Sweet describes this type of leadership:

> A collaborative model is at the heart of the Christian faith. Jesus himself was teamwork-obsessed. He spent his ministry not founding local communities or growing a mega-following for himself, but building a handful of itinerant disciples in first-century Palestine into a great team that could create a culture of perichoretic love. He called his disciples in many cases teams. He sent out his disciples always in teams. This type of leadership is more of a dance compared to a march-in-step hierarchical model.[30]

At Amazing Grace the leadership style is more like the dance characterized by Sweet. All decisions are collaborated upon as a church. It is not a top-down hierarchical model controlled by the pastor. *Although the pastor leads, decisions are placed before God in prayer and the community of leaders discerns what God wants Amazing Grace to do and where God wants Amazing Grace to go.* The voices of those with the gift of discernment, not including the pastor, are given special attention. It is an awesome process to experience.

In the process of discernment the leaders of Amazing Grace want to follow Jesus and they want Jesus to control the church. They realize that the best path is Jesus' way. The leaders of the church relinquish control and power to King Jesus. They have learned that control is the killer of mission in the local church. William Easum, in *Sacred Cows Make Gourmet Burgers*, clarifies this point:

> Established churches worship at the feet of the sacred cow of control. Control takes many shapes; our insistence on controlling everything that happens in our congregations and denominations; our desire to coordinate everything that happens, or to know about everything before it happens, or to insist on voting on every issue in ministry; a parlor that few people use; a gym floor that must be kept scratch free; a kitchen that no one can use except designated persons; money that belongs to the trustees; an official body that has to approve every decision. Control is stifling the spiritual growth of God's people. In the local church, control is exercised by a handful of laity. Within denominations, control is exercised by the clergy. The laity stifles growth in the local church, and the clergy do so within the denomination.[31]

However, not only does the laity have control issues in the local church, but *there are also many pastors who struggle to control everything in the local church. A controlling pastor can also stifle mission into the jails.* One can see the need of health in the local congregation before embarking into jail church planting. Control issues are the greatest dividing factor in the greater Church and the local congregation. It can also destroy the possibility of a local congregation planting a jail church.

The leadership of Amazing Grace has embraced the Lutheran doctrine of the priesthood of all believers. This doctrine states that both clergy and laity are priests of Christ sent to be in mission in his name. Covert writes, "The priesthood of Believers is the presence of Christ in action—people reaching out to others with concrete forms of service. The priesthood is the extension of Christ the healer—those who are willing to suffer in order to help alleviate the pain of others. According to Bonhoeffer, 'The Church is only the Church when it lives in someone else's house, not its own.'"[32] Corporately the disciples of Amazing Grace feel a calling by God to enter into the Maricopa County jail complex and enter into someone else's house, another culture, and a very different world.

Always there has been a sense of excitement surrounding the mission of the jail churches. In the beginning, the jail pastors (those members of Amazing Grace who are pastoring the jail churches) were hesitant and nervous entering into the jail complexes. After the first visit, they realized just how exciting and rewarding this mission into the jails could be. Schwarz explains, "By accepting the mandate for jail and prison ministries—by marching fearlessly past the rows of razor wire and armed guard posts—you are going into the very depths of hell to mine precious gems for the Lord."[33] What seemed frightening at the outset to the jail pastors and some members of Amazing Grace changed into a true delight in a very short time. When Cecilia, a member of Amazing Grace, started jail services she was not sure if she could preach to forty plus inmates by herself. Cecilia was having problems just coping daily with her work and her adult children. Now she preaches to over forty women inmates regularly every Thursday with no guard present. Cecilia is actually finding healing and wholeness in the jail church. The inmates have become precious jewels, sisters in Christ, mined for the pleasure of the King.

Ultimately, the pleasure of the King is what planting jail churches concerns. Amazing Grace entered the Maricopa County jail complex in obedience to Christ's command. It is not about nickels and noses or church growth. For Amazing Grace, planting jail churches is a

way to follow the Way, Jesus. Chaplains Beckner and Park emphasize this point: "Prison (jail) ministry is not an option (Matt 5:36);
it is the heart of our God, the Good Shepherd, who asks us to join
Him seeking, caring for and welcoming home those sheep that have
lost their way."[34] This is the only valid motivation for planting jail
churches.

CHAPTER 2

THE CONTEXT OF THE MARICOPA COUNTY JAIL COMPLEX

The Philosophy of the Maricopa County Jail Complex

The context of the mother church, Amazing Grace, has been examined in detail. This chapter turns to the context of the jail churches in the Maricopa County jail complex. In Maricopa County jails, the system is designed to punish the inmates rather than rehabilitate them. According to Head Chaplain Gregory Millard, *two-thirds of the inmates have not yet been sentenced.*[1] They have not been proven guilty but the jail system starts to punish these untried people upon their entry into the jail system. Sheriff Joe Arpaio, the Toughest Sheriff in America, states that the jails should be an unpleasant place to be:

> Other measures also embody my philosophy of making the entire Maricopa County jail system less pleasant, more efficient and less burdensome on the taxpayers. The bottom line can be summed up in a line I constantly repeat: *Our inmates should never live better in jail than they do outside.* It's that simple. Jail should be a place nobody ever wants to return to.[2]

The philosophy of the Maricopa County jails is to punish and not restore. It is not supposed to be an amusement park. Again the sheriff states: "Save the ones you can save. Help the ones you can help. Control the rest. That might sound harsh to you. I don't know. If it sounds harsh, that's all right, because jail is a harsh place. Jail is not a reward or an achievement, it is punishment."[3] Punishment is the main focus in the toughest jail in America, while rehabilitation and restoration are treated very marginally by the sheriff's office.

The Arizona jails, however, should not be judged too harshly as this attitude of punishment is widespread throughout the United States. Covert explains:

> Although many institutions claim to promote rehabilitation, they remain demeaning environments. Prisoners find themselves in a system that does little to provide the incentives and resources that facilitate personal change. But the problem goes much deeper than apathetic and insufficiently trained staff members—it is rooted in a society whose prison philosophy is revenge and punishment.[4]

The punitive mindset is supported by the voting taxpayers. One person complimented the sheriff saying, "Good for you for cutting out coffee. If it were up to me, I'd have the prisoners on bread and water."[5] The public is the problem. We are the public!

Unfortunately, society wants to punish and does not want it to be expensive. In keeping with societal demands, the Maricopa sheriff's department prides itself on saving the taxpayers money. Sheriff Joe Arpaio declares, "We've had three or four problems with 150,000 people coming through my system—150,000 a year. We run the most efficient jail system in the country. Our meals are down to thirty cents a meal per inmate."[6] Head Chaplain Millard, speaking at an annual training event at the jail complex in October 2006, estimates the Maricopa County jails save $350,000 annually by using religious volunteers to provide services.[7] The Lord uses the state's desire to save money to open the doors of the jails in order to bring the Good News to the incarcerated. However, aside from the financial savings the sheriff calls the religious volunteers his *secret weapon*. The impact the varied religious programs has in calming the jail population is noticeable to the staff. Furthermore, the sheriff realizes that lives are changed through these various programs for the good of society. We are thankful for the opportunity God has given us through Sheriff Arpaio to preach Jesus in the jails! I wonder if Sheriff Joe is aware of how many inmates will be in heaven because of his efforts.

Unfortunately, society and the jail system do not look at inmates as human beings. They are seen as a threat to society who must be treated harshly and cost-effectively. Sheriff Arpaio's description of the inmates evidences this:

> The sad truth is, they don't even respect themselves, having abandoned the most basic of normal, decent feelings and attachments—at the bottom line, too many of these cons don't even value their own lives. . . .That's what crime is all about; that's who criminals really are—cowardly and stupid, contemptuous and vicious. Don't let anyone—the lawyers, media, anyone—tell you differently."[8]

Needless to say, not all of the employees at the Maricopa County jail complex share these beliefs or attitudes. However, I have found these sentiments are dominant amongst the staff. The reader should not be naïve; there are many hardened criminals in the jails. On the other hand, two thirds of the inmates have not been sentenced. They are still legally considered innocent until convicted.

When one enters the jails to minister, one is entering a different world and a harsher world. This is a world that dehumanizes and desensitizes people, whether they are guilty or innocent. Spitale powerfully decries this situation:

> What, one may ask, are men doing in cages? This condition should be reserved for wild animals on display. It becomes even more heartrending when one considers that there is likely more public outcry over animals in captivity than there is for men and women. Something is wrong. How can men and women made in the image of God be reduced to

such a state—a condition that has been traditionally reserved for animals? The devil has come to steal not only our souls but our humanity as well. When you see men and women in cages, the doctrine of sin leaves an undeniable impression upon your mind and leaves little room for doubting its existence.[9]

In the Maricopa County jails inmates are in cages surrounded with razor wire and guard towers. They wear black and white striped uniforms, pink underwear, and pink plastic sandals. They receive two meals per day consisting of bologna sandwiches and a stew-like substance with bread. If they are fortunate they can get a job in the kitchen or chain gang in order to get a break from the boredom. *This is a completely different and dark world compared to the world in which we live, which was created by a loving God.* This is our mission field.

Difficulties in Doing Jail Ministry

There are many difficulties that arise when planting jail churches due to fact that one is entering a different culture. This culture requires the inmates to adapt, as well as those who want to reach these inmates with the gospel. Chaplain Spitale describes prison culture, and his words are applicable to the Maricopa County jail complex. He states:

Prison is another culture. It has its own code of ethics, its own mores and social values. Prisoners have their own language. Words like "PC," "POP," "Max," "kid," "lugged," and a host of other terms are all part of everyday life behind the walls. New ones seem to be added to the list every week; it is impossible to keep up with all of them. Volunteers need to learn the basic, time-tested terms, however, or they will remain in the dark. But prison is more then just a whole new vocabulary; it is an experience filled with different codes of behavior and unwritten laws that define what is acceptable and what is not. It is a mindset, a backdrop that swallows up the inhabitants by degrees, and conforms them to the twists and weaves of its cold, gray fabric. The change is subtle, prolonged for some, stark and frightening for others. To remain as before is not an option.[10]

The inmates become different people when they enter the jail complex. It is necessary to adapt and change to this new culture in order to reach them with the love of Christ.

This new culture is one that features a high density of inmates in the jail complexes. This overcrowding of inmates leads to a change in behavior. Covert states:

> Research concerning the effects of residential density on responsiveness to the social environment is also relevant. Subjects experiencing high density conditions are more likely to withdraw from social interaction with strangers and to have problems relating to neighbors. Residents of high density environments were also less likely to engage in self disclosure, form group consensus, and to help others. The general pattern of these results is that residents of high social density environments engage in withdrawal and decrease their level of social interaction.[11]

One inmate stated that one time during his incarceration, there were six inmates in a cell designed to house two people. The high density of inmates can cause difficulties in reaching inmates on a personal level, which means it will be more difficult to encourage the inmates to attend services and to become part of a jail church.

High density leads to the inmates being suspicious of one another and those who come to minister to them. It is difficult to form a Christian community when suspicion and fear dominate the environment. Covert clarifies this aspect of incarceration:

> Suspicion is a dominant feature of inmate life. Prisoners are inclined to misinterpret situations, mainly because they are looking for ulterior motives in the actions of other people. Suspicion not only damages relationships but also it robs offenders of meaningful opportunities for personal devel-

opment. Inmates have difficulty trusting each other on any level. They know how far they will go to survive in their environment; therefore, they also know the manipulative capacity of their peers. Prison relationships are tense, complex, and always changing. Crowded conditions, diversity and personal struggles all combine to create a community where feelings are unstable. Paranoia is inevitable, and manipulation is a natural survival mechanism. For some residents, survival means withdrawing from the population altogether, while for others it means identifying with those who have power. But no matter what type of friendships a prisoner develops, they all revolve around survival. Inmates do what they perceive is necessary to protect themselves.[12]

In planting a jail church this paranoia must be replaced with trust in Jesus and trust of the jail pastor. This will open the inmates to trust one another to some degree. Complete trust between inmates, however, is very unlikely and also unwise.

Another difficulty is that inmates tend to live one day at a time. It is a matter of survival but it can also damage the inmates socially. Covert describes this condition:

Felons expend most of their energy just trying to cope with the daily stress of incarceration. They struggle intensely to improve themselves in the midst of many obstacles. They try to live "one day at a time," meaning that they must confront basic need issues each day. . . . They are cast into a world with different rules, where distortions and contradictions are the norm. For this reason it is difficult for them to maintain perspective in the present. Because prisoners tend to live in the past, they do not mature socially.[13]

Although the ages of the inmates in the jail churches vary substantially, their overall maturation level seems to be late teens or early twenties. This can be due to a drug or alcohol addiction or to the inmates' lack of education. The focus on their past, maturation level or lack of education is a barrier that can be overcome with the

Good News of Jesus. Jesus can bring them into the present and grant them a future. In light of this difficulty it is understandable that the inmates' favorite hymn is "One Day at a Time."

There are many divisions within the jail population. Covert explains, "Prisons [jails] contain men and women from various cultural, racial, religious, and socioeconomic backgrounds. These distinctions reflect different belief systems and responses. A prisoner's self-perception is understood in the context of his or her background and family influences. Prisoners normally provide support for those who share a similar background."[14] The dominant division of inmates in the Maricopa County jails is race. Inmate Kelly Preiss explained that no matter how well the inmates integrated during worship, when they returned to their pods they separated into racial groups.[15] It is simply a fact of survival.

Erica, a young woman recently released from Estrella jail, gave me a jail vocabulary lesson.[16] The following terms were defined: white men and women are called "woods"; Hispanic women are "pisas"; Hispanic men are "rizzas"; Black men and women are "kinfolk"; the leader of a group is the "head"; the leader's assistant is the "second head"; an advocate is an "advisor"; and a hit man, enforcer, or one who carries out plans, is a "torpedo." In addition, Spitale adds: "Inmates who came from the same neighborhoods or who ran in the same circles are called 'homeys' or 'homeboys.' Gangs in particular, like to use these terms. It identifies them; there is a common loyalty."[17] It is important to learn the inmates' language and social groups in order to be effective in communicating the Gospel.

Another term that is vitally important for jail pastors to know is the word "setup." Schwarz explains, "A setup is a situation where you are forced into compromising your own beliefs, standards, or institutional rules. You are forced or tricked into a compromising situation, and then taken advantage of by an inmate to receive favors or contraband like drugs, alcohol, etc."[18] *A setup can destroy an entire network of jail churches and lead to one's own incarceration.* It is necessary to understand the vocabulary of the jail culture. Jesus says that believers are to be "as shrewd as snakes and as innocent as doves" (Matt. 10:16). These are words to live by in the jail context.

One should look at entering the jail complex as going into a foreign country. This is a foreign country with a very different culture, language, and so on. At the same time, this foreign country can be perceived as enemy territory. Schwarz continues, "By accepting the mandate for jail and prison ministries—by marching fearlessly past the rows of razor wire and armed guard posts—you are going into the very depths of hell to mine precious gems for the Lord."[19] Unfortunately, the jail complex is Satan's home ground.

The Inmates and Families of Inmates

The only demographic information available regarding inmates at the Maricopa County jail complex comes from Head Chaplain Gregory Millard. He estimates that there are ten thousand inmates in the jail complex and that approximately thirty-five hundred of them attend weekly worship or Bible study.[20] There are no demographic statistics pertaining to race, age, and so on. However, many of these inmates have much in common.

Many of the inmates are in jail due to an addiction to drugs or alcohol. Arpaio states, "Almost 70 percent of inmates doing time in America's prisons and jails have been convicted of violating drug laws or because of drug-related crimes. Drugs are not [only] illegal by themselves; they also account for an overall exponential growth in all criminal activity."[21] Hence, those who work with jail churches are generally dealing with addictive and dysfunctional personalities.

At the same time, many of these addicts realize that being incarcerated may have saved their lives and provided the impetus to change. Covert states:

A number of felons feel that their incarceration literally saved them because their luck was running out. In the outside world they lived a life controlled by drugs, crime, and violence. While these prisoners did not actually desire incarceration, they now realize that getting caught saved them from self destruction. For these individuals imprisonment is truly an agent for change.[22]

Most of the inmates who have become members of Amazing Grace are thankful for being incarcerated. They believe it has saved their physical life as well as spiritual life. Kelly Preiss, a 23 year crack cocaine user, served over two years in prison and jail for stealing a 30 pack of beer. He is thankful for being arrested and incarcerated. He says, "It saved my life!" Although incarceration can be a life-saving and life-changing time, it is not easy. Many of the inmates suffer from depression and it affects the entire community.

Depression is evident in correctional facilities, often destroying inmate advancements and potential. Having lost their enthusiasm, perspective, and hope, some felons withdraw into their own world of cynicism. Anger and aggressive behavior also indicates chronic depression. These moods affect the entire institution, leaving the lingering possibility for conflict.[23]

One inmate, a financially secure professional on the outside, shared with me the severe depression that completely immobilized him when first incarcerated at Lower Buckeye jail. Fortunately, he received antidepressants from the jail clinic and was able to survive his time of incarceration. During his twelve months he read over one hundred books to fight off the depression.

In the jail complex not all depression is diagnosed or treated. Many times the jail pastors hear of inmates staying in their bunks and missing worship due to severe depression. Ricardo, an illegal alien, was so depressed about being separated from his wife and five children that he remained isolated in his bunk for over a month. He didn't realize anti-depressants were available. He finally returned to worship after the jail pastor relayed a worship folder to him and Ricardo regained a sense of hope.

Even if the inmates escape severe depression, their emotions are still under constant attack. Covert describes this:

Correctional facilities are molded by the clashes of races, cultures, and religions, where prisoners compete for power, control, and survival. They are neighborhoods of discontent where anxiety and fear translate into mistrust and manip-ulation. As communities separated from society, prisons [jails] function apart from the rapidly changing world, and this environment affects tension levels. A prisoner's social-ization terminates when he or she enters prison [jail]. This abrupt interruption of life, and the loss of support systems that comes with it, are emotionally devastating.[24]

The inmates live in a state of uncertainty and tension. *Their lives are emotional roller coasters that are usually headed in a downward spiral. They are uncertain of their futures and usually during their time, hear many different scenarios by their public defender or the other inmates.*

In this always tense situation many inmates enter into same sex relationships. Chaplain Covert explains:

Imprisonment also causes some offenders who were not previously gay to engage in homosexual activities. This behavior may be a result of sexual insecurity; it may also be a way to relieve sexual frustration, stop threats, or promote personal gain. Although the reasons for homosexual activi-ties vary there is little doubt that such involvements increase an inmate's emotional turmoil, creating new areas of guilt, jealousies, and rivalries. Moreover, these prisoners risk the transfer and spread of disease.[25]

I ministered to a young woman incarcerated in Estrella jail. One day upon visiting her I noticed bruises on her neck. (hickies) She said they were given to her by another inmate. She had engaged in a same sex relationship for her physical safety. I read to her from Romans chapter one regarding same sex relationships and coun-seled her. Eventually, she ceased the same sex practices. Previously, outside of jail, she had attended a church with her husband and young daughters. This woman, like all inmates, was seeking to survive her incarceration.

The inmates are not the only ones who are simply trying to survive. Covert writes, "The family finds its world being pulled in many directions. Like the inmate, family members are also reduced to a 'survival mode' that threatens relationships and order."[26] Schwarz adds, "For every person incarcerated, there are three to five other people affected: mates, children, parents, etc. Inmates and their families, represent a large segment of society in any culture."[27] The separation or disconnection can occur within the family as well as between the inmate and his loved ones. Schwarz continues, "When a family member is arrested it usually creates great anxiety, fear, and uncertainty for their mates, children, or parents. Imprisonment brings a double crisis to a family. The first crisis is that one of the family members has been arrested for breaking some law. The second crisis is that the family is split apart. Losing a family member to imprisonment is similar to the person dying."[28] Cynthia, a Latino homemaker, was left with three children to raise on her own when her husband was incarcerated. This included making a house payment and car payment aside from other normal household expenses. She had to enter the workforce and place her children in daycare. Eventually, she divorced her husband and he is now serving time in prison again. The inmates' families also feel the effects of incarceration.

It is during these times of separation that religious beliefs come to the forefront. H. McCubbin, a sociologist, studied families separated for various reasons.

> The families who participated in McCubbin's study reported that religious belief was an important factor in their ability to manage the tensions of separation, particularly for those experiencing moderate and severe stress. Spiritual support helps maintain the family unit, contributes to individual self-esteem through love and care, and serves as a reference point for norms, values, and expectations that can guide families in stressful situations. Similarly, when all family members believe in God they form a bond of trust with each other.[29]

God becomes more important for inmates and their families during their time of separation. However, as demonstrated by Cynthia and her husband, "It cannot be said that religion alone holds families together or that spiritual people do not terminate relationships. Nevertheless, there is a closer bond and more 'staying power' between people who share a common faith. The testimony of numerous inmates and their families reinforces this truth."[30]

I had the opportunity to minister to a single mother who served two years in Perryville prison for drugs, crystal methamphetamine. During this time I also ministered to her three children and her mother. It was miraculous to see God hold this family together for two years. The inmate's mother returned to the church after many years and one of her grandsons appears to be headed for ordained ministry. The Lord worked in a powerful way through our community of faith at Amazing Grace to help sustain this family. *Furthermore, the family and the church grew exponentially in their faith.* A relationship with God and the fellowship of believers becomes more important to many inmates and their families.

The Opportunities Provided by Jail Ministry

There are many opportunities afforded the Christian Church in the jail environment to minister not only to the inmates but also to their families, the jail employees, and the greater community of faith. The Christian community has the opportunity to exhibit restorative justice in a system, culture, and society that is punitive in nature.

As described above, the goal of the Maricopa County jail complex is to make incarceration an uncomfortable punishment in order to dissuade inmates from returning to jail. The Church has an opportunity to be grace in action for these inmates. Beckner and Park expound on this point:

> Restorative justice is a biblical based paradigm that is founded in a call to the ministry of reconciliation. We no longer see men as the world sees them, but we see them through the eyes of Jesus. Man has committed the crime of high treason against God. The penalty is death. Punishment is deserved, but the great mediator brings justice to the earth. This new justice is not retributive in nature, but redemptive. This justice brings healing to relationships with God and the community of man. Restorative justice is justice that heals relationships. As sin is the primary barrier

between God, man, and his community, so is crime an act that disrupts the peace of the community. The restorative justice paradigm suggests that crime is an injury to the victim, the community and the offender. The goal of justice should be to correct the wrong, the conflict or the injury that has caused the damage.[31]

By being a means of restorative justice or grace, the Christian community can provide healing not only for the inmates but for persons in the community of faith. As the mother church experiences inmates and released inmates who have been restored and freed by the grace of God, that same grace becomes more real and accessible to the members of the church. In essence, the mother church simultaneously finds itself a provider and recipient of God's grace. As inmates experience healing, many members of the local church are freed by social norms to confess their sins and to accept forgiveness and healing. One member, a longtime Lutheran, after hearing the former inmates' openness, now has no trouble sharing his past battles with alcoholism. Not only inmates are being freed by the Spirit, the members of the mother church are also being freed. Don't be fooled, there are more people in bondage in the local church than in many jail churches. Many inmates actually experience more freedom behind bars than people who are physically free in our churches. Many of our church members are captive to drugs, alcohol, sex, anger, abuse, pornography, bad relationships, loneliness, depression, guilt, false guilt, shame, pain, disease, codependency, etc. The list is endless of the hidden chains that captivate so many active church members.

The main focus of the jail churches, however, is to bring the Good News of Jesus to the inmates. In Jesus, the inmates find hope, healing, and connection. Connection is so very important to them, as they have been completely cut off from all they know and love. Spitale writes,

As most people who are caught for a crime they have committed experience, life on the outside is usually interrupted suddenly. It doesn't matter that you have been sharing your life with people whom you love. It doesn't matter that you were in the middle of a mutual routine. Suddenly, you are cut off from them. And, as far as the pain itself goes, it doesn't even matter that you have brought it upon yourself or that the lifestyle you were leading made such a trip almost inevitable; the pain is still there, not only for yourself but also for those you have left behind. If it is a girlfriend, the pain of a sudden, complete separation comes crashing in on you. If it is a wife who has been good to you, it is even worse. If there are children, it is worse still. The greatest pain of incarceration is the forcible separation from those you hold most dear.[32]

While the isolation of incarceration is devastating, jail churches have the opportunity to connect the inmates with Jesus and his body, the Church. In this connection the inmates experience healing and hope within the devastation of their isolation.

Kelly Preiss, who became a member of Amazing Grace while awaiting sentencing, is now incarcerated in a prison in Tucson. Kelly shared that his return to prison this time was different now that he has a community of faith. The last time Preiss went to prison he subscribed to *T.V. Guide* magazine for the sake of receiving some mail from the outside. This time he received mail and visitations from a variety of members as well as his pastors. Kelly survived his time in prison and grew in his faith even though his wife left him and he ended up divorced. Jesus empowered Kelly to get through these trials. Ministry in the jails and prisons gives believers the chance to connect felons with Jesus, a connection they so desperately need.

A loving supportive community can also connect inmates' families with Jesus and help nurture wholeness. Schwarz states, "A church home: The most important thing you can do for an inmate's family is to provide a loving, supportive, accepting church home."[33] This is a serious challenge to the mother church that cannot be taken lightly. If the mother church cannot accept these refugees, then it should not plant jail churches. *Many of the inmates and their families have been hurt in the past by the church. To provide the inmates hope of restoration while incarcerated and then to reject them or their families upon release is counterproductive. The church actually may find itself driving people away from Jesus.* The church is called to love all people to Christ. It cannot pick and choose those whom Jesus has called. The inmates know what is real and will not remain in a church that rates them as second class citizens. They have been judged and found lacking their entire lives. It is not our place to judge. Jesus' words in Matthew 7: 1-5 apply to us:

"Do not judge, or you too will be judged. For in the same way you judge others, you will be judged, and with the measure you use, it will be measured to you. Why do you look at the speck of sawdust in your brother's eye and pay no attention to the plank in your own eye? How can you say to your brother, 'Let me take the speck out of your eye,' when all the time there is a plank in your own eye? You hypocrite, first take the plank out of your own eye, and then you will see clearly to remove the speck from your brother's eye."

Another opportunity to witness the grace of God is to the staff of the jail complexes. Beckner and Park write, "Christians should carry themselves as professionals throughout their work in all the institution. Therefore, they should carefully know and observe all the rules of the institution, understand well the culture (both officers and inmates), and understand and respect all the lines of authority under which they are privileged to minister."[34] By obeying the rules of the Maricopa County jail complex, the members of Amazing Grace provide witness to the authority of Christ in their lives. This also preserves the integrity of the jail churches. Prison Chaplain Schwarz writes, "A good volunteer will follow every rule in the institution. The rule may seem stupid, but he is happy to submit himself to it. One volunteer can destroy an entire program by not obeying the rules."[35] Jail pastors serve Christ but as a privilege granted by the county sheriff. In this respect, jail pastors and volunteers must follow the words of Christ: "Give to Caesar the things that are Caesar's" (Matt. 22: 21).

The Detention Officers

No one can affect the immediate success of a jail church as much as the detention officers (the "DOs") in the jail context. Although the officers are considered "the enemy" to the inmates, they cannot be perceived in this light by the jail pastors. Beckner and Park explain,

> To most inmates, the correctional officers are the bad guys!
> . . . [Continually being the bad guys] often reveals or ampli-
> fies existing difficulties in [the DOs'] lives, such as conflicts
> with spouse or children, difficulty meeting financial obliga-
> tions, problems with abusive speech toward inmates and
> co-workers, problems with authority and impatience with
> anyone who makes their job more difficult. This means a
> volunteer desiring access to inmates may be perceived at
> worst, as a problem, and at best, as an inconvenience.[36]

It is very easy for jail pastors to side with the inmates against the DOs. After all, the inmates are the members of their congrega-tions. But this is a mistake because the DOs are largely in charge of expediting worship in the jails. Worship can be delayed or greatly diminished by choosing to battle the DOs.

Furthermore, the DOs are also part of the mission field. Beckner and Park explain,

> One of the most common errors religious volunteers make
> is neglecting staff in order to minister to inmates. The truth
> is that approaching the staff with wisdom and sensitivity
> will only enhance your ministry to inmates. . . .Understand
> their struggles. Many of the staff are hurting because correc-
> tional work is very stressful. It is routine, lonely and often
> unpleasant. Work is unappreciated and typically unrewarded,
> both financially and in terms of visible results. Correctional
> staffs are not highly paid nor do they receive positive feed-
> back from the inmates.[37]

The DOs should be viewed as an opportunity to minister and witness to the love of Christ. They are not simply barriers to be overcome. One inmate from one of Amazing Grace's jail churches helped encourage two guards (DOs) to start attending church again with their families. I have been privileged to meet Christian DOs in the jails and to pray for them and their families. *By and large the DOs are professional and appreciate the efforts of our jail pastors.* There are few exceptions.

The DOs also serve to keep the jail volunteers focused in reality. The reality is that the inmates are generally felons and not all of them will come to know Jesus and his love. Shaw writes, "In other words, officers are apt to see incarcerated men at their worst, whereas chaplains [or jail pastors] are apt to see them at their best. Unless chaplains [or jail pastors] keep reminding themselves of things as they actually are, they are liable to go starry-eyed and too idealistic to be of any practical help to those who really mean business about becoming rehabilitated."[38] The DOs are a constant reminder of jail pastors and volunteers' context for ministry and can make us more effective servants of Christ.

The Current Jail Churches

In 2006, Amazing Grace planted two jail churches in the Lower Buckeye jail for men which Widney and I served as jail pastors. I served with and trained Widney for four weeks and then turned these two jail churches over to him as his flock. By 2007, the Lord had raised up two new female jail pastors, Lydia and Cecilia.

Amazing Grace planted one new jail church in the Estrella jail for women with Lydia serving as pastor. She was trained by Widney and me. Later this same year, another jail church was added in Estrella with Cecilia serving as pastor. Cecilia was trained by Lydia. Unfortunately, in 2007, Widney found it necessary to cancel one jail church due to health issues. This is the foundation in place for planting additional jail churches.

Currently, Amazing Grace has three jail pastors and three jail churches. The jail church in the Lower Buckeye jail ministers to approximately twenty-four inmates per week. The two jails in the Estrella jail minister to approximately seventy inmates per week. Amazing Grace is planning on planting two to three new jail churches in 2008 in the Durango jail and training three new jail pastors. One of the new jail churches will conduct worship services in Spanish. Amazing Grace has experience in the Maricopa County jail complex and a good reputation with the staff and inmates.

PART TWO:

THEOLOGICAL FOUNDATIONS

CHAPTER 3

THEOLOGICAL CONSIDERATIONS FOR CONVERSION/RENEWAL

There are many theological considerations in planting churches in the Maricopa County jails. The jails are a very different type of mission field. Several aspects of Scripture and the gospel initially motivated me to begin planting jail churches. Others surfaced in my understanding after planting and participating in the jail churches. It has truly been an amazing adventure.

The Call to Make Disciples

In the Gospel of Matthew, Jesus commands, "Therefore go and make disciples of all nations baptizing them in the name of the Father and of the Son and of the Holy Spirit and teaching them to obey everything I have commanded you. And surely I am with you always to the very end of the age" (Matt. 28:19-20). He commands us to go to "all nations." The greater Church has had no problem going to foreign lands to obey Jesus' great commission. In fact, the Church has even applied this to the new building developments in the suburbs in America. In recent years, however, the Church has not been consistent in obeying the Great Commission in regard to the cities. The institutional Church has fled the cities for the financially secure suburbs. Lesslie Newbigin observes:

69

In a situation of declining numbers, the policy has been to abandon areas (such as the inner cities) where active Christians are few and to concentrate ministerial resources by merging congregations and deploying ministers in the places where there are enough Christians to support them. Needless to say, this simply accelerates the decline. It is the opposite of a mission strategy, which would proceed in the opposite direction, deploying ministers in the areas where the Christian presence is weakest. The large-scale abandonment of the inner cities by the mainline churches is the most obvious evidence of the policy that has been pursued.[1]

The cities are growing in population but not growing churches due to lack of a mission strategy. This is the same with outreach to the incarcerated. As stated above, *there are between one thousand and two thousand jails throughout the United States in need of jail churches.*

Just as the cities are growing so is the jail population growing. This ministry book offers a strategy that focuses on mission in the jails, however, this mission also can and will affect the urban mother church. *The Maricopa County jail complex houses approximately ten thousand inmates and has its own unique culture. The jail complex is a world unto its own.* The Maricopa County jail complex is to be included in Jesus' "all nations." According to Head Chaplain Millard, approximately thirty-five hundred of the ten thousand inmates attend a worship service or Bible study in a one-week period.[2] There is a tremendous need for the Church to go and preach the Good News to the incarcerated in the Maricopa County jails but also to those in prisons and jails across America. Shaw writes, "The nineteenth century account *Prison Secrets* records a Quaker inmate at Ludlow Street jail saying: 'The doctrine of the chaplain mayn't be mine, but I tell thee, he brings the only sunlight that comes into this dark corner of iniquity.'"[3] Jesus commands believers to go and bring light into the darkness of the incarcerated. If the church shirks its responsibilities then the Mormons, Jehovah Witnesses, and Moslems, are more then willing to stand in the gap. Eternity lies in the balance.

Furthermore, Jesus specifically commands us to go to the incarcerated in the parable of the goats and sheep. Matthew writes,

> Then the righteous will answer him, "Lord when did we see you hungry and feed you, or thirsty and give you something to drink? When did we see you a stranger and invite you in, or needing clothes and clothe you? When did we see you sick or **in prison and go visit you?**" Then the King will reply, "I tell you the truth, whatever you did for one of the least of these brothers of mine, you did for me" (Matt 25: 37-40).

Believers will be judged on our effort or lack of effort to reach out to those who are incarcerated. Jesus calls them his brothers. This mission is not optional. Chaplain Shaw states, "My chief concern is that God spoke in the book of Matthew that, when he was in prison we didn't come to see about him. And further on, he breaks it down, letting us know he means everybody who is in prison."[4]

This mission strategy may not be beneficial financially but the rewards are tremendous as believers follow Jesus and obey his commands. Beckner and Park state:

> We must follow Christ's example, by being willing to sacrificially give, expecting nothing in return. In fact, our reason for doing so must not be the needs of the prisoner. **It must be obedience to Christ.** If our ministry ever becomes ruled by needs, we will surely become overwhelmed and burn out. However, if we give ourselves to God and freely give out what He has given to us; then what we have to give is something valuable, life changing, and "non-draining." In 2 Corinthians 1:3, 4, Paul says, "Blessed be God who comforts (graces) us in our trials so that we may be able to comfort others with the same comfort that we ourselves are comforted of God."[5]

One takes this mission on in obedience to Jesus and not for financial gain or prestige. In the process, those who enter the jails and prisons will see others transformed by Christ and also will experience this transformation in their own lives. This ministry is about the life-changing relationship in Christ for all involved.

Nominal Christianity: The Necessity of Conversion/ Renewal of the Inmates

Many of the inmates in the Maricopa County jails were raised in the Church.[6] They were baptized, received their First Holy communion, and were confirmed. *However, in all these religious practices, the inmates never had a relationship with Jesus or became his disciples. The Church has failed to make them disciples. They are Christians in name only.* Hence, they are "nominal Christians" according to Eddie Gibbs:

> A nominal Protestant Christian is one who, within the Protestant tradition, would call himself a Christian, or be so regarded by others, but who has no authentic commitment to Christ based on personal faith. Such commitment involves a transforming personal relationship with Christ, characterized by such qualities as love, joy, peace, a desire to study the Bible, prayer, fellowship with other Christians, a determination to witness faithfully, a deep concern for God's will to be done on earth, and a living hope in heaven to come.[7]

In regard to this oversight by the Church, Dallas Willard writes, "And this with its various consequences is the Great Omission from the Great Commission."[8] The greater Church has focused on making members of the institution rather than followers of Jesus. One of the results is the need for jail churches.

At one of Amazing Grace's jail churches, there was a worship leader who was incarcerated. This young man could play the piano and guitar and had a professional-quality voice. Although he had actually been paid to lead worship in a church prior to his incarceration, he never had a relationship with Christ. He was never discipled. He confessed that he was an intravenous drug user who was a Christian in name only. He also believed that God sent him to jail and later prison to save his life. He became a disciple of Jesus at the jail church.

In part, the Church is responsible for the incarceration of these children of God. The greater Church has been too focused on making members instead of disciples (that is, committed followers of Jesus). Pastors have been trained to count nickels and noses rather than mentor disciples for Christ. Willard explains:

> He (Jesus) told us, as disciples, to make disciples. Not converts to Christianity, nor to some particular faith and practice. He did not tell us to arrange people to get in or make the cut after they die, nor to eliminate the various brutal forms of injustice, nor to maintain successful churches. These are all good things, and he had something to say about all of them. They will certainly happen, if—but only if—we are (his constant apprentices) and do (make constant apprentices) what he told us to be and do. If we just do this it will little matter what else we do or do not do.[9]

Jesus calls believers to make committed disciples, lifetime apprentices for him, both inside and outside of the jails.

Inside the Maricopa jails, as stated above, approximately half of the inmates are nominal Christians. The other half of the inmates hold beliefs ranging from atheism to neo-paganism. Most inmates, in one way or another, have had bad experiences with Christianity and/or the Church. Hence, *the inmates need to be converted to Christ or renewed in their faith. They need to be loved to Jesus. Once they encounter the living Christ through believers, they can then be discipled.* Willard continues, "The language of the Great Commission, in Matthew 28, makes it clear that our aim, our job description as Christ's people, is to bring disciples to the point of obedience to 'all things whatsoever that I have commanded you' (Matt. 28:20)."[10] The commission in the jail churches is to make disciples who have been changed by the love of Christ and not simply to make church members. Glen Stassen, in his book, *Authentic Transformation*, declares, "Martin Luther and Jonathan Edwards emphasize regeneration, as cleansing the springs of action, as freeing the Christian to love, and as a conversion from distrust to trust in God. Conversion transforms not only our basic trust but also our loyalty and faithfulness to that taught and embodied by Jesus Christ."[11] The jail churches will emphasize faithfulness and loyalty to Jesus as his disciples and not as future members to the mother church.

Indeed, Christianity without commitment is religion and not relationship with Jesus. Furthermore, a church without commitment is a religious social club and not the Body of Christ. The jail churches will strive to make committed disciples of Jesus and committed churches for Jesus.

Relationship versus Religion

Jesus said, "And surely I am with you always to the very end of the age" (Matt. 28:20). In this verse Jesus is describing an ongoing relationship with his disciples after he ascends into heaven. This relationship is deeper than the one Jesus shared with his disciples in his earthly body. In this new relationship, Christ will live in and through his followers. In the parable of the vine and branches, Jesus says, "Remain in me, and I will remain in you. No branch can bear fruit by itself; it must remain in the vine. Neither can you bear fruit unless you remain in me. I am the vine; you are the branches. If a man remains in me and I in him, he will bear much fruit; apart from me you can do nothing" (John 15: 4-5). George Hunter III describes this relationship:

> This is the supreme promise of the Bible—that we shall all know God, that we shall know the forgiveness, acceptance and love of God, that we shall have this new covenant written upon our hearts, that we shall be born anew from above and shall know the power of God and the life of eternity within us and among us. This faith relationship with God comes to us by sheer grace; we can never deserve it or earn it because we are all sinners.[12]

This relationship is what must be emphasized in the jail churches or any mission field for that matter. *It is in this relationship that the inmates can be changed by God and live with him.* Ultimately, this is what saves them now and in the age to come. Teresa, a female inmate, writes,

But the main idea or point is God saved me and He knows I have a purpose in life. . . . I love God so much; I never thought I could have such a wonderful relationship with a man. I found the man I have been looking for my whole life. It is God! . . . I am a new woman and I can't wait for my family to see me. I can't wait to live life with God. I never did this. I am so excited!

This is what the mission of the jail churches is about. The jail churches want people to enter a faith relationship with God.

One's faith relationship is vertical, that is, between oneself and God. However, one's faith relationship is also horizontal, including others. Jesus finishes the parable of the vine and branches by stating, "My command is this: Love each other as I have loved you" (John 15: 12). The loving relationship disciples have with God is to overflow to others. Covert clarifies this concept:

Ministry in prison can only be successful when the believers become part of a priesthood, touching one another's lives with a sensitive presence of compassion and support. By participating in such a ministry we heal others, and at the same time heal ourselves. Ministry to other people has a miraculous way of alleviating our own pain, which applies directly to the daily needs of prisoners.[13]

This horizontal love of God takes place in the jail churches. The inmates are changed and their relationships with one another are changed. At the same time, those who pastor and volunteer at the jail churches are changed. Joaquin, a Latino inmate, in a prayer request card from March 2008, describes this love: "I would just like to let you know that now that I've got close to God, my days are more beautiful! And I feel happy. I would like to pray for everybody's family and their health and for my Mom and my family. Thanks to God I'll be getting out soon. Thank you, Jim Widney [jail pastor]." *Jail ministry is about a loving relationship with God and with one another. It is not about religion or religious doctrine.*

The Inmates as Fertile Soil

"On hearing this, Jesus said, 'It is not the healthy who need a doctor, but the sick. But go and learn what this means: I desire mercy, not sacrifice. For I have come not to call the righteous, but sinners'" (Matt. 9: 12-13). Jesus makes it quite clear that the church's mission is to sinners, the lost, the unsightly, and the imperfect. Logan and Cole affirm, "Bad people make good soil; there is a lot of fertilizer in their lives."[14] Unfortunately, the greater Church has lost sight of this mission. The greater Church seeks out those who are comfortable and financially capable of supporting the local congregation. This excludes urban areas, jails, prisons, Latino missions and any area that has "bad," broken, or financially broken people.

If one will accept the mission to sinners and the outcast in imitation of Christ, then the jails and prisons are a great place to begin. The jails and prisons are filled with sinful and broken people. The inmates have, in many cases, hit bottom and they know they need God. They have tried everything else life has offered and ended up incarcerated. Spitale states:

> I find the majority of prisoners have been humbled to one degree or another and tend to be honest about their spiritual condition. I am not saying that they are all humble but they have been humbled. They are honest about their need and their own inability to make their lives work. No wonder the Lord finds such fruitful vines growing in this vineyard! Many on the outside are still wrapped in the prideful cloaks of their outward appearances, possessions, and social positions in life. But inmates have had all that stripped away from them. And it has turned out to be a marvelous grace.[15]

For many inmates being incarcerated serves as their salvation in this world and the next. One female inmate, in a letter to Jail Pastor Lydia Brockman from February 2008, writes,

> My life from May to end of July was nuts. I saw horrible things, did things I never in a million years would ever think I could do or would want to do. So when they put the cuffs

on me, all I could say was, "Thank you." . . . I have never truly accepted God in my life ever. But when those cuffs hit my wrists I knew right then that God saved my life. Out of all the horrible things I did this is what I was getting arrested for. God did this for a reason. He knew I needed Him. And I found Him.

This is common in the Maricopa County jail complex. Many inmates have shared with their jail pastors the redemption and salvation Jesus has given them through incarceration. The inmates are extremely hungry for God. Chaplain Spitale states emphatically:

I do not know of any more fertile ground for the gospel in all the United States than our jails and prisons. I make the statement unequivocally and without reservation. If you are looking for a more fruitful harvest field, apart from leaving the country, you will be hard-pressed to find it. I received this letter from an inmate in Florida: "Our largest home mission field with the greatest need seems to be our prisons and jails. Of course some of the absolute best Christians I have met are behind fences and walls and will be for the rest of their lives. Praise God he uses us no matter where we are or what we have done!" Think of the following scenario: Where else can you find so many for whom the facade of self-sufficiency has been stripped away? Where else can you enter a place that is filled from top to bottom with people who know they have done wrong and, in most cases, readily admit it? Where else can you find so many broken, hurting, lonely people all collected together in one small place? Where else can you enter a community where so many of its members have been humbled? . . . Where else can you enter an arena where every unbeliever understands that your function is to talk about God? And further, that they expect you to bring Him up?[16]

If the Church is ready to embrace the mission to sinners who know they are sinners, then the harvest is more than ripe in the jails and prisons. *Jesus commands his disciples to go into this darkness to bring the outcasts his light. Jesus has put down the gauntlet, and it is up to the Church to obey.*

The Weakness/Foolishness of God

Saint Paul writes to the church at Corinth,

> Brothers, think of what you were when you were called. Not many of you were wise by human standards; not many were influential; not many were of noble birth. But God chose the foolish things of the world to shame the wise; God chose the weak things of the world to shame the strong. He chose the lowly things of this world and the despised things—and the things that are not—to nullify the things that are, so that no one may boast before him. It is because of him that you are in Christ Jesus, who has become for us wisdom from God—that is, our righteousness, holiness and redemption. Therefore, as it is written: "Let him who boasts boast in the Lord" (1Cor. 1: 26-31).

These verses highlight one of the aspects of Luther's theology of the cross.

In the Heidelberg Disputation, Luther describes the hidden way that God works in the world. He writes, "That person does not deserve to be called a theologian who looks upon the invisible things of God as though they were clearly perceptible in those things which have actually happened [Rom. 1:20]. He deserves to be called a theologian, however, who comprehends the visible and manifest things of God seen through suffering and the cross."[17] Luther is stating that God works in many unexpected ways as demonstrated by Jesus' death on the cross. Luther would also point to the virgin birth as another mysterious work of God. God will most likely use people and things one would least expect to accomplish his tasks. Stassen states, "We cannot come to the end of the road our rethinking the ideas of power and omnipotence . . . His power is made manifest through weakness and he exercises sovereignty more through crosses than thrones."[18] *It is in the crosses of the incarcerated that one can see the paradox-*

ical way God works in the world. The inmates in the Maricopa jails (these men and women who have been discarded by the world and declared "unclean") are now becoming God's chosen instruments. Beckner and Park explain,

> Yet this plague has produced a paradox! The same substances that have led so many into a life of crime have produced a brokenness that is bringing many of the same to Christ. Prisons and Christian recovery centers are producing a massive crop of men and women who are healing and responding to the call of God in their lives. A literal army is being raised up from the "valley of dry bones" of substance abuse. God has breathed new life into them and they are rising from their graves ready to become soldiers in a new spiritual movement. There are signs that we are on the threshold of a new reformation where ex-offenders and recovered addicts will play a major role in this army God is raising up. Once, God chose a nation imprisoned in Egypt to become a "nation of priests" to the world (Exod. 19:6). Paul declared, "God has chosen the foolish things of the world . . . the weak . . . the base . . . the things despised by the world and things which are not to bring to nought things which are" (1 Cor. 1:27-28). God has always chosen people who were "not a people" to populate His Kingdom. One need only look at the leaders of criminal justice and recovery ministries today to see outstanding illustrations of this principle. The Lord is raising up a great army that were previously impaired but now are repaired and prepared for the coming great harvest.[19]

I have witnessed firsthand the changes in inmates, the changes in the guards, the changes in the mother church, and the changes in me. These changes all came about through the Holy Spirit using inmates, former criminals, as his chosen instruments. *We are always good enough to be used by God!* Bill Yount, a prison volunteer for over twenty years, shares a very powerful vision pertaining to the unexpected way God works:

Then I saw Jesus standing in front of seemingly thousands of prisons and jails. The Lord said, "They have almost been destroyed by the enemy, but these souls have the greatest potential to be used, and to bring forth glory to my name. Tell my people, I am going this hour to prisons to activate the gifts and callings that lie dormant in these lives that were given before the foundations of the earth. Out from these walls will come forth a spiritual army that will have power to literally kick down the gates of hell and overcome satanic powers that are holding many of my people bound in my own house. Tell my people that great treasure is behind these walls, in these forgotten vessels. My people must come forth and touch these lives, for a mighty anointing will be unleashed upon them for future victory in my kingdom. They must be restored." . . . When I saw the golden shields, I heard God say to these warriors (former inmates), "Now go and take what Satan has taught you and use it against him. Go and pull down the strongholds coming against my Church." The spiritual giants then started stepping over the prison walls with no one to resist them, and they went immediately to the front of the battle with the enemy. I saw them walk right past the church and the big-name ministers—known for their power with God—(they) were surpassed by the giant warriors like David going after Goliath! They crossed enemy lines and started delivering many of God's people from the clutches of Satan while demons trembled and fled out of sight at their presence. No one, not even the church seemed to know who these spiritual giants were or where they came from. They were restored to God's house and there was great victory and rejoicing. I also saw silver, precious treasures, and vessels being brought in. Beneath the silver and the gold were the people nobody knew: rejects of society, street people, the outcasts, the poor and the despised. These were the treasures that were missing from His House. Then the Lord said, "If my people want to know where they are needed, tell them they are needed in the streets, the hospitals, the missions, and the prisons. When they come there, they will find Me and the next move of My Spirit."[20]

Every jail pastor, chaplain, religious volunteer or church member involved in prison or jail ministry that I have worked with can testify to the truth of this vision. *Once again, the Lord is using the foolish and despised things and people of this world to bring more and more people into the kingdom. I believe the released inmates will be the tip of the spear in the new reformation. The old walls are coming down and God is doing a new thing.* No one can boast. It is the Lord Jesus who is doing this new thing.

The Power of Prayer and Inspirational Worship

Luke writes in the book of Acts, "They devoted themselves to the apostles teaching and to the fellowship, to the breaking of bread and to prayer . . . And the Lord added to their number daily those who were being saved" (Acts 2:42 and 47b). Luke is describing the early Church and the phenomenal growth both spiritually and numerically the Lord provided. The movement was centered in the elements of worship including the apostles' teaching, fellowship, and the Lord's Supper, and prayer.

Worship and prayer are the two factors that can effectively grow disciples and grow and multiply churches. In regard to worship, Stassen contends,

The Christian faith must therefore always center upon gathering the congregation around its head, nourishing and strengthening it by immersion in the revelation of God contained in the image of Christ, spreading it not by dogmas, doctrines and philosophies but by handing on and keeping alive the image of Christ, the adoration of God in Christ. So long as Christianity survives in any form it will always be connected with the central position of Christ in worship. It will either exist in this form or not at all.[21]

Jesus is the center of worship just as he is the center in a disciple's life. In worship, inmates and all people should experience the life-changing presence of Jesus. In his book, *Church Next*, Eddie Gibbs writes, "In true worship God is the audience, and the congregation are the participants. Worship is the wellspring of our witness."[22] Worship is a powerful tool God employs to bring people into a relationship with him.

Prayer is also essential in every mission field. Walter C. Hobbs, in his chapter titled "Dependence on the Holy Spirit" in *Treasures in Clay Jars*, writes,

> Missional churches know that trouble will surely batter them; indecision will plague them; evil will terrorize them. . . . The early churches knew this well (Acts 21:5), and just in case they might forget it they were often reminded by the apostles (see 1 Thessalonians 5:17). Prayer was essential to the people of God in their mission of carrying Good News to the nations. It still is. The missional church is incapable of fulfilling its call, save for guidance from the Holy Spirit of God and for the Spirit's empowerment of the church's witness to that reality.[23]

Without the power of the Holy Spirit through prayer, the Church is simply an empty vessel. Prayer paves the way for mission and ministry.

Jail churches and their mother churches must make prayer a priority. *Prayer is not and never has been an aside in the Church in mission. Prayer is at the core of mission.* Stassen asserts, "Prayer [is] not for show, but for God's will to be done and for deliverance to come. Prayer includes facing the evil that is in us. It asks to be allowed to participate in the drama of grace and deliverance in which it is God, not us, who is the chief protagonist."[24] Through prayer God changes people, both the one who prays and the one prayed for. Spirit-guided prayer and Christ-centered worship are essential for church growth and spiritual growth.

The Contagious Nature of Conversion/Renewal

Paul writes, "I will make you envious by those who are not a nation" (Rom. 10: 19). In this verse Paul is describing how he wants to make his own people, the Jews, jealous or envious of the Gentiles who have accepted Jesus as the Messiah. Through this envy Paul hopes and prays that the Jews will embrace Jesus as the Messiah, the Christ of God. This happens in the jails and prisons as well. Inmates observe Christian inmates closely and become envious of the changes in their lives. Even in a jail setting transformed Christian inmates exhibit peace, patience, and love, and the other inmates want it. Covert states, "In correctional facilities, inmates observe Christians more than any other group. They want to ascertain if Christians are different: whether they really have inner peace, spiritual strength, and love. Therefore, the church must develop a strong priesthood in prison communities. Christian inmates are the primary communicators of the gospel and the main support system for their peers."[25] The inmates are God's primary instruments in bringing people to Jesus. The other inmates are always watching.

Jail churches simply initiate the discipleship multiplication process, and the inmates then take over with Bible studies and prayer circles in their pods. The jail churches empower the inmates to be active disciples of Jesus. Covert continues,

As members of the church, inmates must be taught that they are valuable in God's kingdom. They need to see their environment as a mission field, recognizing that they reside in a community that is accessible to few outside Christian workers. Prisoners should be encouraged to move beyond their own pain in order to touch the lives of those around them. In this way, prisoners not only minister to other people, but their actions become a channel of grace for them. Any ministry that only addresses individuals without emphasizing the need for community nurturing and mutual healing will never be strong, and in time it will fade away. In every penal institution there are individuals with special gifts that, when developed, can be a blessing to others. No one can identify better with prisoners than their peers, and those who have been spiritually transformed are unquestionably the most effective communicators of the gospel and witnesses of the new life in Christ.[26]

The transformed non-judgmental lives of the inmates arouse the envy of the other inmates. Fischer declares,

> Ever been around new believers? They are wide-eyed with amazement. They lap up everything they can get. They feel like they have such a long way to go, but they are happy to be on the right road, nonetheless. There is innocence to their learning and yearning. It would be unthinkable for them to apply a teaching to anyone but themselves because a new believer assumes everybody else knows more than they do. They are the antithesis to the Pharisees in every way.[27]

This contagious aspect of new Christians reaches even beyond the walls of the jails.

Although the inmates are effective in making disciples inside the jails, they are equally as effective upon their release. One inmate, upon his release, brought his family and friends into the church. This same inmate witnessed to an unchurched bus driver and invited her to church. This bus driver eventually joined the church, participated in a Cursillo retreat, and recommitted her life to Jesus. She went on to lead her dying husband to Christ on his deathbed. In essence, she wanted the same thing this enthusiastic inmate demonstrated for her husband and herself. *The contagious aspect of new Christians is one of the many theological considerations that surfaced in the planting of jail churches.* This has led to organic or natural church growth and multiplication. I was astounded at the impact released inmates had on Amazing Grace. (This is clarified in Chapter Seven.)

CHAPTER 4

A THEOLOGY OF CHURCH PLANTING IN THE JAILS

Definitions of "Church" and "Pastor"

Saint Paul writes, "Now you are the body of Christ, and each one of you is a part of it. And in the church God has appointed first of all apostles" (1 Cor. 12: 27-28a). It is clear from Paul's words that the Church, or the body of Christ, consists of people. *The Church is people. It is not a building or a location but the Church consists of followers of Jesus gathered together in various places.* Paul also makes it clear that Jesus alone is the head of the Church. Os Guinness states in his book, *Dining with the Devil: The Megachurch Movement Flirts with Modernity,*

> If Jesus Christ is the head of the church and hence the source and goal of its entire life, true growth is only possible in obedience to him. Conversely, if the church becomes detached from Jesus Christ and his word, it cannot grow however active and successful it may seem to be . . . The authentic movements in the church are those that are set in motion by God's decisive authority, especially the decisive authority of grace."[1]

The Church is the people of God empowered by the Holy Spirit under the authority of its Head, Jesus Christ, to be a means of grace to the world. Easum declares: "The head of the Body is Jesus Christ. It is our commitment to the Lordship of Jesus Christ as the head of this body that binds us all together. When Jesus lives in us, His DNA is imprinted within us. We are made a new creature."[2] Wherever the followers of Jesus Christ gather, this is the Church. The geographical location or type of physical structure is inconsequential to the being of the Church. Hence, it is accurate to describe the jail ministries as jail churches. Smelly inmates gathered in black and white stripes, pink underwear, pink sandals, and leg chains or pink handcuffs are the church, the Body of Christ.

In addition, the members of the Church share a vertical relationship with Jesus and a horizontal relationship with one another. This horizontal relationship is ever expanding as the Church reaches out to others with the love of Christ. Hunsberger writes, "The fruits of the missionary movement and the emergence of a global church have led us to see that the church is essentially a body of people sent on a mission."[3] In this book, the mission starts with the mother church (in this case, Amazing Grace) sending jail pastors to the inmates in the jails. As these inmates receive the word of God and are transformed into disciples of Jesus, they then become the members of the Church in mission in their respective pods. Therefore, the inmates become a body of people sent on a mission. They are, or become, the Church in the Maricopa County jails.

When I started outreach into the jails, I thought it was simply a jail ministry. Soon, I witnessed the inmates laying on hands and praying for one another. Then the inmates went back to their pods and invited other inmates to church. They formed prayer circles and Bible studies in their pods. The inmates began singing hymns of praise to God and celebrating the Eucharist in their prayer circles. *I realized this was not simply another jail ministry. This was the Church, alive and in action. Perhaps these jail churches are even more alive and active than many churches outside the jail complex.* Chaplain Spitale states,

Inmates don't have the privilege of choosing which church they would like to attend, as we on the outside do. If a member of a church on the outside doesn't like the service, or a pastor, or some other member of the congregation, he can leave and go somewhere else. (And evidenced by the amount of church-hopping that seems to take place, it seems to be a freedom many a disgruntled member chooses to exercise.) But inmates don't have that choice. Their church is the church in that prison [or jail], like it or not. This means that they have the opportunity to display the unity of Christ in a way that is seldom achieved, even on the outside. What an irony that Jesus is accomplishing this unity in institutional chapels across the country, and he is doing it with prisoners, many of whom are baby Christians at that![4]

Jail churches are indeed churches and not just ministry outreaches. Many local churches and pastors could learn what it means to be the Church from the jail and prison churches, as the jail churches have had a unifying and edifying effect on Amazing Grace.

The purpose of the jail church is the same as the purpose of the mother church and the greater Church. Easum states: "The purpose of the church is to win the world to faith in God through Jesus Christ. . . . The goal is never simply 'to run the church,' no matter what size the church may be."[5] The purpose has not changed in two thousand years. At Amazing Grace and the jail churches, this purpose has been simplified to "love all people to Christ." This is their purpose and mission.

With the development of the jail churches, the religious volunteers sent into the jails became more than just lay people. They served as pastors to the inmates. Many people would protest, stating the jail pastors' lack of educational training and academic credentials prohibit them being called "pastor." Schwarz contends, however, that "jail and prison ministry is a supernatural ministry birthed in the heart of God. It is a ministry in which one must be anointed, appointed, chosen, called, and sent. It must be done in the realm of the Spirit in absolute obedience to God's will. When the Lord calls us to this ministry He gives us His very own burden, love and compassion of His Holy Spirit. It is a special ministry and precious to Christ."[6] One must remember it is Jesus who extends the call to jail ministry and not the mother church or senior pastor. Jesus is in control and he usually calls the most unexpected people to be jail pastors. It never ceases to surprise me the broken people Jesus uses so effectively in the jails as jail pastors. At the same time, these broken vessels discover healing in a hell hole.

Easum describes this phenomenon: "Equipped laity replace ordained clergy. . . . Clergy are no longer set apart due to ordination. Pastors are sought with the ability and passion to share their faith with others regardless of academic credentials. Emphasis on ordination is replaced with an emphasis on the ministry of all believers."[7] This applies to the jail churches. While in the jails, the jail pastors serve as pastors to the inmates. When the jail pastors return to the mother church, they are disciples who serve as jail pastors. This is a new paradigm for the local church in regard to understanding pastors and the church.

Church Multiplication/Organic Development

Saint Paul writes, "Now you are the body of Christ, and each one of you is a part of it" (1 Cor. 12:27). The church is made up of people and those people make up the body of Christ. Robert Logan and Neil Cole, in their book, *Raising Leaders for the Harvest*, explain, "The Church is organic, a living thing. Every analogy given for the Church is of a living and dynamic nature: a bride, a body, a flock, a vine, a field, a growing mustard seed, a harvest, even a building made with living stones."[8] For example, a healthy physical body grows and changes and reproduces. In the same way, a healthy church grows and changes and produces other churches. In turn these churches, which have the same healthy DNA, will grow and change and reproduce more healthy churches. Logan and Cole define this genetic code or DNA: "This is the DNA of Christianity: Love God; Love others; Make disciples as you go."[9]

This is described as organic development. Logan and Cole continue, "Organic development happens 'all by itself' (Mark 4:26-28). It is a flexible and adaptable process, the result of a divine partnership with God. Organic development is simple and reproductive;

the most important characteristic is God changing lives."[10] Organic church development is a movement of God. It is God using healthy churches, which are made up of people, to birth other churches. This leads to church multiplication and not simple church addition. In this way entire communities and eventually the entire world can be won for Christ. The traditional method of the church hierarchy or the institutional church planting churches in selected areas is simple addition. When each congregation can birth additional churches then church multiplication can occur.

In *Be Fruitful and Multiply*, Logan writes, "Church multiplication movements can happen anywhere, anytime. They adapt to the cultures, they raise leaders from the harvest, and they build multiplication into the genetic code [DNA]."[11] Hence, a church multiplication movement can even happen in the Maricopa County jail complex and has already begun. I have witnessed continued multiplication of jail churches and small groups in the jail complex. The multiplication simply flows and is birthed in the heart of God. Logan and Cole state, "A movement is the result of God's grace pouring out locally. Align yourself with what God is already doing in your community."[12] This is exactly what Amazing Grace is doing as it plants additional jail churches. Hopefully, this strategy will be adopted by other healthy churches. Logan and Cole explain that, in order to take a movement from the micro level to the macro level, the following steps must take place: multiply disciples; multiply leaders; multiply churches (authentic communities); multiply movements.[13]

The strategy here is to establish a model that will lead to the multiplication of further movements in other churches and other jail complexes. In fact, at Amazing Grace this multiplication has already begun. Recently, two new jail pastors began serving (who are members of a church that serves with Amazing Grace in the jails) and already several inmates have expressed their desire to become pastors. Furthermore, many jail inmates who are sent to prison are taking this "Christian DNA" with them. Kelly Preiss, now in prison, has started a Bible study and inspired two prison officers to start attending church with their families outside the prison complex. Once God's kingdom comes there is no containing it. As Roland Allen states, "The great things of God are beyond our control."[14] *As a result of its success in planting jail churches, Amazing Grace has recently been led to plant a mission church in Flagstaff, Arizona. Once church planting starts, multiplication develops naturally.*

Effective Evangelism

The most important aspect of effective evangelism is to be authentic; believers must get out of their comfort zones and go. Logan and Cole declare, "Our reaction to the world of today should be a Church that says we are coming to you, just as we are. We must move toward a missional or incarnational model, rather than a model that says, Come to us."[15] In recent decades, the Church has focused on bringing people to the church building or a church program. *In the postmodern culture, the Church must go to those who have not heard the good news and make Christ known to them. The Church can no longer be complacent and hope that the Lord will send people through their doors.* Jesus' command was "Go" (Matt. 28:19). He did not tell his disciples to wait until someone showed up at their doorsteps.

In addition, the disciples went as they were and they went everywhere. Jesus instructed his disciples when he sent them out: "Take nothing for the journey except a staff, no bread, no bag, no money in your belts. Wear sandals but not an extra tunic" (Mark 6:8). Jesus is encouraging them to travel lightly, and simply to go as they are. He implies that they should be who they are. They are fishermen, tax collectors, and sinners. Jesus did not dress the disciples up to be Pharisees or Scribes. Jesus wanted these men to be authentic. In the same way Jesus wants those who plant jail churches to be authentic. Mike Gardner, a former inmate who is now on probation, spent time with me when he was first released. After a month, he decided that Christianity was real because I was real. Another inmate, Teresa, affirms this point in a letter she wrote to one of the jail pastors, Lydia, in April 2008: "God has moved in your life, and because of you and your life story, I know he will do the same for me. I truly believe God saved me! He rescued me and put me here for a reason." Effective evangelism is authentic and always on the move.

Effective evangelism is focused on a relationship with Jesus Christ. It is not a matter of being the most popular jail pastor or largest jail church. It is not a matter of having large numbers of released inmates joining the mother church. Evangelism is getting people attached to Jesus and not to a church leader or member.[16] Saint Paul tells the Corinthian church, "It is because of Him (God) that you are in Christ Jesus, who has become for us the wisdom from God that is our righteousness, holiness, and redemption. Therefore, as it is written: 'Let him who boasts, boast in the Lord'" (1 Cor. 1:30-31). An inmate's relationship with the jail pastor and mother church will eventually end. But an inmate's relationship with Jesus will last forever and lead to life. *The Church enters the jails for Jesus and not out of personal interest.*

Evangelism focuses on the main thing, Jesus, and not on unique doctrines accepted by the mother church. This is true in the greater Church but even more so in the jail churches. Spitale expounds,

> What volunteers should keep in mind is that their participation at any chapel service is also under observation. Special attention given to any inmate is noted, as is attention given to doctrinal issues that have tended to divide Christians. Don't forget that this is their [inmates'] only church. We don't want to find ourselves before the Lord as having been the reason for dividing his body. It becomes essential that we do not bad-mouth other Christian volunteers in any way, even if we have differing doctrinal issues. It is also important that we do not make our pet doctrines an issue for division. Focus on the essentials. There are many beautiful fish in this aquarium.[17]

Pet doctrines will not save anyone inside or outside the jail complex. Saint John exclaims, "And this is the testimony: God has given us eternal life, and this life is in His Son. He who has the Son has life; he who does not have the Son of God does not have life" (1 John 5:11-12). Evangelists need to focus on Jesus and the essentials of faith.

Nevertheless, many inmates will come to faith in Christ because of their relationships with the jail pastors or other inmates. Usually, the horizontal relationships with others lead to the vertical relation-

ship with God. Logan states, "People come to God through relationships."[18] Timothy came to Christ through his grandmother, his
mother Eunice, and Paul (1 Tim. 1:5). Henri, a bilingual Latino
inmate, brought other Latinos who could not speak English to one
of the English language jail churches. He acted as their interpreter
and as a result one of these Spanish-speaking inmates was baptized
at the Lower Buckeye jail. Many other inmates have received Christ
due to the ministry of jail pastors. Evangelism is relational.

Effective evangelism can start with and is enhanced by authentic
transformation in the church. Logan and Cole write, "Changed lives
can spark a momentum within the church."[19] This happened in Saint
Paul's life. In the book of Acts Luke writes,

> When he (Paul) came to Jerusalem he tried to join the disci-
> ples, but they were afraid of him, not believing he was really
> a disciple. But Barnabus took him and brought him to the
> apostles. He told them how Saul on his journey had seen
> the Lord and that the Lord had spoken to him, and how in
> Damascus he had preached fearlessly in the name of Jesus.
> So Saul stayed with them. . . . Then the church throughout
> Judea, Galilee, and Samaria enjoyed a time of peace. It was
> strengthened; and encouraged by the Holy Spirit; it grew in
> numbers living in fear of the Lord (Acts 9:26-31).

When inmates see other inmates praying, reading their Bibles,
and at peace, they begin to ask questions. Eventually, their desire
for peace brings them to the jail churches. Beckner and Park concur,
"When a prisoner can actually see someone's life change from bad
to good that creates hope deep inside his or her heart and soul. Then
the Holy Spirit's allowed to come in and then you can look at the
more serious Christian teaching."[20] Evangelism in the jail churches
is sparked by changed lives. This is something the greater church
needs to learn. *True evangelism involves the Holy Spirit, power, and
transformation of the individual and the church.*

Naturally, effective evangelism is driven by a sincere passion
and compassion for the lost, those who do not know Jesus. Saint
John states, "We love because He (Jesus) first loved us" (1 John

4:19). Disciples see those who need Jesus with the eyes and heart of Christ. Furthermore, they are excited because they can show those without Jesus the Way, the Truth, and the Life. Logan and Cole explain, "Realize there is a party in heaven when just one sinner repents! We've got to get as excited about this as God gets!"[21] Effective evangelism is passionate about Jesus and bringing people to him!

Due to the vast difference between the jail culture and the culture outside of the jails, evangelism in the jails must be extremely flexible. The key is to follow the Spirit's leading. Logan and Cole instruct, "Adapt to the steady wind of the Spirit. There are many ways to catch hold of the Spirit's wind within your culture, whether it is windsurfing, sailing, or hang gliding."[22] Evangelism in the mother church and the jail churches must always be open to doing things differently and adjusting to the flow of the Spirit. Saint Paul sets the example when he states, "I have become all things to all men so that by all possible means I might save some" (1 Cor. 9:22). Evangelism has been flexible from the beginning of the Church. The Spirit cannot be contained in one model of evangelism. Flexibility needs to be the rule and not the exception, especially in an urban context and in the jails. *Style is not as important as content. The content is always Jesus!*

Reproducing Disciples

Jesus' command is, "Therefore go and make disciples" (Matt. 28:19). The disciples were commanded to reproduce disciples. Logan and Cole define a disciple as "one who has a loving devotion to Christ, His Church, and the Great Commission."[23] The jail churches will seek to make disciples and not simply enroll members. Logan and Cole expound, "Discipleship should actually begin before a life transformation or conversion. New Christians hear God's word before they accept Him. . . . Therefore, all discipleship practices should begin with the lost and not with the found."[24] The goal is to make the inmates passionate about Jesus and their relationships with him. This passion will lead the inmate disciples to make other disciples.

Hence, a multiplication of disciples will occur rather than a simple addition of inmates. Logan and Cole explain,

> The reason that groups and churches multiplied in the New Testament is because the first generation Christians were obeying a very specific command—*to make disciples!* When Christians are obedient to this single command, it results in the multiplying of groups and churches. To multiply churches and groups without multiplying disciples is not only disobedient, but it is also nearly impossible![25]

Reproducing disciples is mandatory in any church planting strategy. Multiplication starts with the smallest unit which is an unchurched person and expands naturally. One inmate at Lower Buckeye jail was transferred to the Towers jail within the county jail complex, where he started a Bible study attended by forty-five inmates. This is unplanned natural church growth.

The question arises regarding whom a believer should choose to disciple. The candidates for discipling usually come from the harvest or mission field. Logan and Cole write, "The criteria for selecting disciples: (1) A recognized need for Christ; and (2) Faithful to the disciple-making process"[26] Everyone in a jail church meets these criteria. They come to worship because they know they need God and generally they will be faithful to the process due to their limited activities. Spitale describe these inmates: "The average prisoner sitting in his or her cell isn't really interested in lofty opinions about theology. 'My life is broken. How do I fix it?' is the basic question he asks. 'If you say it's God, tell me how that works.'"[27] The harvest is very ripe for discipling in the jail churches. The incarcerated are hungry to know Christ!

Jail pastors do not generally have an excess of one-on-one time for making disciples. Hence, the jail pastor must try to influence a group of fifteen to forty-eight inmates in tight quarters in order to disciple a few. The most effective way of making disciples is the incarnational model. Just as the Son of God put on flesh to save humankind, believers must put on Christ to save others. Logan and Cole exhort, "Since DNA [genetic code for discipleship] can only properly be passed on in a relational setting, it is vital for the lead pastor to incarnate the message by demonstrating it to his core team. More is caught than taught."[28] Inmates must see Christ in the jail pastors in order to be discipled. It is of the utmost importance that the jail pastors demonstrate a healthy Christian model. *Discipleship is contagious.* Many jail pastors from Amazing Grace have heard from inmates that they are different from other religious volunteers entering the jails. The inmates say the pastors' relationship with Jesus is authentic. They want what the jail pastors have. Unbelievers inside or outside the jails recognize Jesus' disciples.

The unbelievers also know if disciples are authentic in their relationships with Christ. In the jails, inmates see other inmates change over time and become more Christ-like. This can prove the effectiveness of one's witness. Spitale declares, "But again, time is a convincer. There are many strong Christians living out their lives with faithfulness and conviction in front of other prisoners. The proof is when you hear the other residents giving testimony to the integrity of a particular Christian inmate. Then you know this inmate's faith is deep and consistent."[29] Kelly Preiss is an example of such transformation. Previously an inmate in Lower Buckeye jail and now in prison, members of Amazing Grace consistently hear reports of his faithful discipleship from staff, other pastors, and inmates.

Ultimately, discipleship is about transformation. Logan and Cole contend, "Transformation is the key for any church. Since the fall of Adam and Eve, we have become beings with a drive to serve ourselves, rather than God. The supernatural aspect of God taking the heart of a self-centered and transforming it into a heart of love and forgiveness is miraculous. It is the basis by which the person receives God's DNA through birth and repentance."[30] This transformation is the proof and fruit of discipleship and it is only produced by God. God reproduces disciples and transforms them. Only God can change the human heart. No matter how successful a jail church may be in reproducing disciples, in the final analysis the jail pastors have nothing to boast about. *The process has been God's from start to finish. The jail pastors and mother church can boast of being used as God's instruments but all is for His glory. Reproducing disciples and multiplying leaders are movements of God.*

Multiplying Leaders

After the inmates have started the journey of discipleship and transformation, it is then necessary to find leaders in order to have a multiplication movement as opposed to simply addition. The leadership comes from the harvest. Logan and Cole write, "New converts are the raw material for leadership selection."[31] This model was established by Jesus when he called his twelve apostles. He did not go to the temple or a rabbinical school when he chose his leaders. Logan and Cole explain, "Jesus didn't look for existing competency in His leadership recruits. He wasn't looking for pre-trained, ready-to-run leaders. If so He would have looked to the ranks of the Pharisees or Sadducees."[32] The leaders for the multiplication of churches in this strategy will come from the inmates. The inmates will lead the expansion of small groups in the pods and eventually plant churches.

Most likely, these leaders will start by planting churches outside the jail complex because upon release they have to wait before becoming jail pastors. In accordance with the sheriff's policy, an inmate must wait twelve months to return as a jail pastor if convicted of a misdemeanor and thirty-six months if convicted of a felony.[33] Realistically, it will take approximately three to five years for an inmate to return to the county jails as a jail pastor. Amazing Grace is over two years into the process and still has not had an inmate return to preach inside the jails. There have been many released inmates anxious to return to the jails as jail pastors. They are hungry to pass on the blessing. The inmates will begin as leaders in their pods, then lead outside the jail, and then eventually return to the jails as jail pastors.

The decision process for selecting leaders begins by looking for a person of peace. Logan and Cole define a person of peace as: (1) Responsive to the message you bring; (2) Relationally connected to all in the pocket of people; and (3) Renowned in reputation"[34] There are inmates who stand out to other inmates. Kelly Preiss and Henri Hernandez (both mentioned above) are excellent examples of persons of peace. They serve as God's magnets, attracting others to Jesus. Covert describes these persons of peace: "As the extension of Jesus Christ, human lives should be holy examples of God's infinite love and transforming grace. Those who are in Christ [Kelly and Henri] will draw others to His saving and sustaining grace."[35] There are many inmates like Kelly and Henri bringing people to Jesus in the jails and prisons. These inmates may spend their entire lives incarcerated and drawing others to Jesus. *When some of these inmates are released and return to a local congregation, however, there will be an explosion of renewal and revival outside the jails. These Spirit-filled persons of peace cannot be contained.* It will take time for the multiplication to happen but, when it does, it will happen in places and churches and people who may never enter the doors of Amazing Grace. Julio, a Latino inmate and illegal immigrant, wants to become a pastor when he is returned to Mexico. Perhaps he will plant a church in Mexico as a result of being discipled by one of Amazing Grace's jail churches. The opportunity in the future for widespread news of Jesus inside and outside the jails is exponential!

The Role of Preaching, Worship, and Prayer

"They devoted themselves to the apostles' teaching and to the fellowship, to the breaking of bread and prayer . . . And the Lord added to their number daily those who were being saved" (Acts 2:42, 47). These were the practices of the early Church that the Lord blessed. In the jail churches, the apostles' teaching comes in the time of worship. Although the inmates study God's Word in the pods, the main opportunity for a dynamic group experience of the Word is delivered in the preaching of the jail pastors. This is a powerful means of grace. The message is always simple. Spitale clarifies this point:

> Ultimately we represent Jesus. We bring our heavenly Father's words of hope and forgiveness, the Son's compassion, and the encouragement and comfort of the Holy Spirit. Our task is to enter the lives of inmates with wisdom and compassion and always to be pointing to the cross. It was at the cross that Jesus died. And for all those who believe in Him, it is at the cross that their death occurred as well. A death to the old

person, and with it, all the slavery to anger's dominance, yea to sin's dominance, has forever ended. Anything that falls short of that message just plain falls short.[36]

This message is preached by Amazing Grace in its jail churches. The jail pastors preach with the intention of making disciples for Jesus. There is a transient trend in the jail population. Generally, they are in jail for six months or less. *Therefore, the jail pastors strive to impact the inmates every time they preach. There is a sense of urgency.*

This sense of urgency is also exhibited in the worship or the breaking of bread and fellowship. Worship in the jail churches, explain Logan and Cole, consists of "exhaling: confessing and cleansing from sin . . . [and] inhaling: implanting and continuing in God's Word [and sacrament]."[37] Once again, although this exhaling and inhaling are practiced in the pods by the inmates, these actions have a different impact when the community is gathered, a sermon has been preached, and the Lord's Supper is received. A time of prayer for confession and forgiveness is offered at every jail church as is Holy Communion. In regard to the breaking of bread in worship, Hunter states, "Wesley even saw the Eucharist as a converting ordinance and welcomed seekers to find the gracious presence at the table and altar."[38] The jail pastors from Amazing Grace agree with John Wesley and celebrate the Lord's Supper at every worship opportunity. I have always seen bowed heads and tears when the Eucharist is celebrated in the jails.

The same is true of prayer. *Prayer is the fuel that empowers churches inside and outside the jail complex. Prayer precedes worship, is part of worship, and goes on continuously after worship.* Logan describes this type of prayer in his book, *Be Fruitful and Multiply*:

Multiplying churches—churches that storm the gates of hell and set captives free—is a spiritual battle fought on a spiritual plane. The stakes are high, the enemy is determined, and we are not strong enough to overcome him alone. God must be with us if we are to succeed. Through prayer and the renewing of our minds, we can tap into the power of the Holy Spirit to change hearts and breakdown strongholds. Prayer is the essential foundation upon which multiplication movements are launched."[39]

This is the type of prayer employed in the mother church and the jail churches. It is daily, continuous, growing, and empowering. Without the heartfelt prayers of God's people at Amazing Grace and in the jail churches there would be nothing to write about. There would be no ministry at all. The practice of prayer in the jail churches and surrounding the jail churches will be discussed further in Chapters 5 and 6.

Baptismal Practice and the Lord's Supper

Baptism and the Lord's Supper are two gifts to the Church from Jesus about which Christians have many and varied views. This section will focus on a theology of practice in the jails pertaining to these two ordinances. Generally, in church growth and multiplication it is considered wise to baptize quickly.[40] In the jails this is true in some cases but not considered the best practice in other cases. In my experience even the jail chaplains are divided on this. For example, in Lower Buckeye jail, the chaplain prefers to baptize quickly and requires a simple written profession of faith. In the Estrella jail, however, the chaplain would rather have the inmates baptized at the inmates' home churches after release in order to promote an ongoing relationship with Jesus in a community of faith. She too will baptize with a written profession of faith but she does not encourage baptism in the jail.

The mother church leaves this decision up to the inmates and their jail pastors. It is preferred to wait for the inmate's release in order to baptize in a home congregation unless the inmate is going to prison. If the inmate is going to prison then it is best to baptize the inmate quickly rather than risk the lack of follow-up in the prison they are moved to. The inmate can also be baptized immediately if he or she has a strong desire to be baptized and consults the chaplain. This calls for a great degree of flexibility and may go contrary to one's congregational polity. Individuals should use communal discernment (as offered in Chapter 6) and they should be open to the Spirit's leading.

The same process of discernment is necessary for the Lord's Supper in the jails. Once more, flexibility is required due to the importance of this special meal to the inmates. Chaplain Covert correctly defines this importance:

> The incarcerated claim, that the Eucharist is a special blessing to them. Many prisoners report that when they meditate on the wounds of Christ, they experience an emotional and spiritual bonding with God. Their experiences parallel the feelings of others who have prayerfully entered into an intimate fellowship with Christ. But prisoners seem to engage in deeper levels of meditation and thanksgiving than those who live in the free community. Their past lives and present circumstances influence their experience. Participation in the Eucharist is a mystical, yet concrete, way of internalizing the suffering love of our Lord. Through silent meditation and reflective prayer, we experience a spiritual touching of Christ's wounds. Also, the broken bread and the wine enable us to probe our own brokenness and find strength in the power of the risen Christ. Eucharist brings forgiveness through oneness with Jesus Christ. Another dimension of the Eucharist is Christian unity, which is vividly communicated when individuals from different backgrounds come together to celebrate as members of one body. This mystical communion reveals that there is one spirit and one church. In fact, the Holy Spirit can bring together the multitude of differences that are found in humanity. This diversity, united through the one Spirit, manifests the creativity, beauty, and power of almighty God; and unity provides a strong witness of his transforming presence in the world. The extremes found in prison [jail] communities make the Eucharist a crucial force of ministry. In the fellowship of Holy Communion, there is a love and equality that tears down the many barriers that separate people. Through this sacrament we realize the power of diversity found in Jesus Christ; we come to under-

stand the church is a mystical communion that can only be made through the Spirit of Christ. This truth should lead us to examine our inner lives, which is yet another dimension of the cross.[41]

The jail churches of Amazing Grace celebrate the Lord's Supper at every worship opportunity and encourage inmates to partake of the sacrament in worship as well as in their pods. *I invite every inmate to the table whether they believe the bread and wine are physically the body and blood of Christ, a symbol, or a real presence of Christ in the meal. Everyone is invited whether or not he or she is baptized. I have witnessed the power of the Spirit working through this sacrament to change individual inmates and form a community of believers within the jails. The inmates become brothers and sisters in Christ through the table fellowship.* Needless to say, this does not necessarily agree with my polity's communal practices, but I have personally felt led by the Spirit to practice in this way. Covert writes, "There is no right way to 'do' church."[42]

Obstacles to Jail Church Planting

The obstacles in the context of the jails that can hinder church planting are the pastors, the inmates, the culture, and the DOs. Logan and Cole state, "We have found the biggest blockage to the growth and multiplication of the church is the pastor."[43] This is true in planting jail churches as well as churches outside the jail complex. The pastor of the mother church is most likely to pose an obstacle at the beginning of planting by withholding permission, delaying implementation, or micro-managing. Later, the jail pastors can stifle planting in the pods and in the jail complex by inappropriate behavior, legalism, neglect, or control. As the senior pastor of a mother church and a jail pastor, I have seen the need for flexibility and trust of empowered individuals to be the main factors in overcoming the pastor as an obstacle.

The inmates can be obstacles if they are not sincere about growing spiritually. They can disrupt services and church planting movements. Shaw explains,

The total involvement of religionists and organizations with the inmate and all of his problems has one drawback, one that everyone recognizes. It invites con and deception by insincere inmates hunting ways to secure their needs or obtain assistance in their efforts to regain their freedom. Outside religionists and organizations promising to become totally involved with the inmate and assisting him with all his problems create a situation ripe for exploitation by criminal and insincere inmates. The only requirement is that they ride the religious pony and, given their basic criminality, deception comes easy.[44]

This can happen within the jail context and it even carry outside to the mother church. In my experience, one inmate, named Donald, was one such individual. Upon release, Donald started attending worship at Amazing Grace. He seemed to be a passionate new convert and a great evangelist. However, after several lies to other members and to me, and hundreds of dollars later, it was discovered that Donald was a con artist. *He was playing Christian for what he could gain from manipulation and deceit.* He was very good at deception. It was a craft that, sadly, he had learned at a very young age and developed into an art. Fortunately, Donald did not destroy Amazing Grace or any jail churches.

Understanding jail culture and learning to adapt to it can be difficult for new jail pastors; yet, this is exactly what the Lord Jesus has called believers to do. In fact, Jesus modeled this by becoming a 200 percent person. Sherwood Lingenfelter and Marvin Mayers, in *Ministering Cross-Culturally: An Incarnational Model for Personal Relationships*, explain, "The point is that Jesus was a 200 percent person . . . He was and is 100 percent God. Yet, Paul tells us that Jesus took the very nature of a servant, being made in human likeness. He was 100 percent human. When He spoke of himself, he called himself the Son of man, identifying completely with those to whom he was sent."[45] Jesus calls believers to do the same. They are to meet people "where they are" with the Gospel of Jesus Christ. The world behind the fences and razor wire of the jails is extremely different from the world in which most people live. Inmates come into worship with black and white striped uniforms and chains on their legs. New jail pastors have to be ready for this obstacle and be a 200 percent person.

The DOs are another obstacle in planting jail churches. The main obstacle they pose is limiting the number of inmates that come to worship. If the jail pastors fill out the appropriate form regarding the performance of the DOs, this obstacle can easily be overcome to some extent. The sergeants can change the DOs' behavior through reprimands and so on. However, the DOs can always bring just enough inmates to worship to get by. I have seen this happen on many occasions when the DO brings forty inmates for a service designated for fifty. Meanwhile, inmates who want to worship are left in the pod wondering why they cannot attend worship. Consistently low numbers at worship can cause a new jail pastor to quit or the chaplain to close the jail church.

The physical obstacles for jail church planting are the pastors, the inmates, the culture and the DOs. However, all these obstacles are created by Satan. He does not want any new churches planted inside or outside the jails. Peter warns all church planters: "Be self-controlled and alert. Your enemy the devil prowls around like a prowling lion looking for someone to devour" (1 Pet. 5:8). His presence may be more pronounced in the jails but the devil can also raise havoc in the mother church. In light of this spiritual opposition, a strategy for planting jail churches will be explored in the next section.

PART THREE:

STRATEGY AND ASSESSMENT

CHAPTER 5

BIRTHING A JAIL CHURCH

Birth a Vision out of Prayer

It is essential to start with prayer when giving birth to a vision in commencing new jail churches. Jonathan Edwards states, "Before God has something very great to accomplish for His Church, it is His will that there should precede it the fervent prayers of His people."[1] The birthing of a vision for jail church planting out of prayer is a two-pronged approach. It involves one's personal prayer life and focus as a pastor as well as the corporate prayer life and focus in the church. In the pastor's personal prayer life, there is a need to focus more on the harvest and listening to God rather than doing all the speaking. Personally, I have always prayed for a harvest, but in the past my motives have been misguided and sinful. I have always sincerely wanted to bring people to Christ but I believe there was also an ulterior motive of growing the numerical size of the church. In addition, since Amazing Grace joined LCMC, I have wanted to plant sister churches for the new association. It is lonely being the only LCMC congregation in Phoenix. *The focus, however, must always be loving people to Jesus with no ulterior motives.* Loving people to Jesus has become my main focus since the adventure in church planting began almost three years ago, and all church planters should strive to do likewise.

After praying and processing over the past three years, my personal vision for Amazing Grace in regard to church planting has evolved. My vision is to be a parent church and to have at least a dozen jail churches planted in the Maricopa County jail complex in the next three years and one church plant outside the jails within four years. Needless to say, these churches will embrace and love all people to Jesus. They will be disciple-making churches characterized by the love of Christ, love for one another, prayer, confession, and evangelism. These jail churches, with the support and coaching of the parent church, will multiply disciples and additional jail churches.

Eventually, as the inmates/disciples are released, they will either join the parent church or, if in a different geographical location, they will join other churches. The vision is that these individuals will plant new churches in the future. It is hoped that disciples of the parent church, the jail churches, and the church plants outside the jails will be willing to risk greatly to advance the kingdom of God. Their focus will always be outward to others and upward to God. This vision seems to be God-breathed because it is so much "outside the box." The vision employs jail churches and jail disciples eventually planting churches outside of the jail complex. Hopefully, the third generation of churches will be outside of the jails. The vision also includes having over two hundred members of the parent church involved in the daily prayer ministry. *The prayers of the parent church and the jail churches will undergird everything that takes place in church planting.* The psalmist declares, "Unless the Lord builds the house the people labor in vain" (Psalm 127:1).

As the vision continually evolves it must be agreed upon by the council and communicated to the church so ownership of the vision is shared and not the sole vision of the pastor and council. The vision has already been shared with the congregation of Amazing Grace and all are extremely excited about this move of the Spirit. The church, council, and jail pastors are all supportive of and praying for this vision. In fact, Amazing Grace's vice president was very excited about church planting and volunteered to head up the team. The reason the council and parent church are open to this vision is because the church's DNA is correct. Love, discipleship, evangelism, and ever-changing adventure are four words that describe the church. Likewise any church that is healthy and has the right DNA (its members love God, love others, make disciples as they go) will be excited about planting jail churches. It must be remembered, however, that the vision and mission are all undergirded with continuous prayer. There are no shortcuts. (See appendix D for schedule of necessary steps) Without prayer, the multiplication of jail churches is impossible.

Prayer Cover (Intercessors): Inside and Outside

In my first three years at Amazing Grace, most of my time has been spent re-inventing the church and making sure the church has the right DNA. Thus far, the church has been successful. In fact, in the last three years the church has successfully planted three jail churches with the same genetic code as that of the mother church. Amazing Grace began a multiplication movement, and recently has started the process of birthing more jail churches. *Amazing Grace is unique in that it reaches out to people other churches generally do not want, including the incarcerated and their families; noisy, badly behaved children; illegal aliens; Spanish-speaking people; convicted felons; the mentally disabled; divorced persons; addicts and recovering addicts; unmarried cohabitating couples; poor people; and the like.* The church has a prayer chain consisting of approximately sixty members for immediate prayer requests and a daily prayer ministry consisting of approximately 130 people. These members pray daily for the church, the jail churches, the pastors and their families, the jail pastors and their families, and for other members assigned to that particular day. This vital ministry always needs to be updated and the focus of the harvest and visioning needs to be reinforced in the prayers.

At the same time, Lydia, a jail pastor, started a prayer service on Monday nights specifically for the mother church and jail churches. Although the service agenda fluctuates, generally it consists of a private time of prayer and confession, followed by Holy Communion, and then a time of prayer walks and corporate prayer. Some people pray sitting, some kneeling, some walking, some prostrate on the floor, some aloud, some quietly, and some in tongues. The atmosphere is similar to the Tuesday night prayer meetings described by Pastor Jim Cymbala at his congregation, the Brooklyn Tabernacle:

> As the meeting edges to a close, I overhear mothers petitioning for wayward children . . . men asking God to please help them find employment . . . others giving thanks for recent answers to prayer . . . tearful voices here and there. I can't help but think, *This is as close to heaven as I will ever get in this life. I don't want to leave here. If I were invited to the White House to meet some dignitary, it would never bring the kind of peace and deep joy I sense here in the presence of people calling on the Lord.*[2]

The prayer service at Amazing Grace lasts between one and two and a half hours. It is an extremely powerful ministry of the mother church that has led to the expansion of existing ministries (e.g. Girl Scouts, Boy Scouts, and Angel Kids) and the creation of new ministries (jail churches and a Christian daycare).

At Amazing Grace, updates and prayer concerns must be regularly communicated to the Monday night intercessors, the prayer chain, and the daily prayer ministers as well as to the church at large. *The mother church must also include the church planters/jail pastors in their daily prayers.* Cymbala explains, "The devil is not terribly frightened of our human efforts and credentials. But he knows his kingdom will be damaged when we begin to lift up our hearts to God."[3] These men and women serve as the point persons/planters behind enemy (Satan's) lines. Schwarz recommends the following prayer list for the incarcerated:

1. The chaplains of the institution.
2. Individual inmates.
3. Families of inmates.
4. The warden [Sheriff Joe] and administrative staff.
5. Correction officers. Safety for prison [jail] volunteers entering the institution.
6. Parolees [probationers]: For their spiritual and practical needs—jobs, housing.

7. Revelation knowledge to meet the needs of inmates.
8. Spiritual revival.
9. For God to raise up strong spiritual leaders within the prison [jail] church body.
10. Inmate prayer requests: Many prison [jail] chapels have a prayer request box. Inmates write out their requests and put them in the box for the chaplain and volunteers to pray specifically for their concerns.[4]

These are recommended requests but it is not a mandatory model. Once again, flexibility is a must. This list simply assists the prayer intercessors who are outside the jail context and it represents some of the many people and things they pray for.

Inside the jail context, the inmates need to be taught and encouraged to pray. Cymbala states; "He [God] wants us to meet the enemy at the very point of attack, standing against him in the name of Christ. When we do so, God will back us up with all the resources of heaven."[5] Amazing Grace has initiated a prayer connection with the inmates at the Lower Buckeye jail, the Estrella jail, and the three churches in the Durango jail.[6] These are point of attack. At the churches in the Durango jail, inmates fill out prayer request cards that the jail pastors pray over and then distribute to the members of the parent church at Sunday worship. Amazing Grace members then take the cards home and pray for these inmates. One senior member of the church, Hazel Spencer, keeps all the prayer requests she receives and prays daily for these inmates. Some of her cards are two years old.

Another element of the strategy is recognizing the needs of the target group through prayer. Through the process of prayer, the intercessors have learned that there are many people who are completely blind spiritually both outside and inside the church. In the jails, the prayer team has discovered many wounded souls who are hitting bottom and searching for hope. Some of these hurting people are repeat offenders that are facing serious prison time. They want love and understanding and joy. They want to be able to laugh and have fun again. They need Jesus. They need the prayers of the church. *Prayer is a disciple's most powerful tool.*

At the same time, from among the inmates come some of the most powerful intercessory prayers of the church. *The impact of an inmate's prayers for a jail pastor is powerful. Often there are tears when the jail pastor realizes that a particular inmate understands his or her needs.* Being a Christian is about focusing on the other person and not on the self. Many times I have been surprised to hear follow-up inquiries about previous prayer requests I have made of the inmates. They are concerned and tell me they have been praying all week for me. It is extremely humbling to be prayed for by a person in chains. Personally, without the inmates' prayers it would be difficult to do all that is necessary in this mission field. It is a heavy load and one of the most difficult tasks is discerning who can be a church jail planter or pastor.

Discerning Who Will Be a Jail Pastor

At Amazing Grace the leadership team for the jail ministry is already in place (see Figure 1).

Figure 1. Leadership Team for Jail Ministry

- Team organizer/leader = Jim Widney
- Interviewer = Robyn Bezanson
- Team communication/computer work = Darol Olson
- Prayer coordinator = Pastor Rick Bezanson
- Council liaison = Lydia
- Team members/ex-inmates = Kelly Preiss and Mike Gardner
- Point Persons = Paul Scott, Bryant Walton, Prisca Walton, Jaime Gomez[7]
- Parent church pastor = Pastor Rick Bezanson

The interviewer, Robyn, interviews prospective jail pastors or point persons using the Church Planter Profile questions found in *Beyond Church Planting* by Logan and Cole.[8] In addition, the use of communal spiritual discernment, developed by Gordon T. Smith, is employed by the leadership team. Smith is Academic Vice President and Dean of Regent College in Vancouver and draws on the teachings of Ignatius Loyola, St. John of the Cross, Jonathan Edwards, John Wesley, Martin Luther and John Calvin.[9] The church council at Amazing Grace employs this method and has found it to be a blessing. In making decisions in the church it is always best to seek God's advice. This is particularity true in choosing a church planter, or in this case, a jail pastor. Logan emphasizes the importance of this task: "The number one reason why churches fail is getting the wrong planter. Planter selection is crucial."[10] Although the process of spiritual discernment is not perfect due to the human element, it does enhance the chances of choosing the right person to plant a jail church.

Within Smith's teachings there are six factors for communal spiritual discernment: humility, consolation, scripture, prayer, (in) community, emotion and reason, and together (in community). The first of these, spiritual discernment, is founded in Jesus' words that "My sheep know my voice, and I know them. They follow me" (John 10: 27). Spiritual discernment involves hearing the voice of the Good Shepherd Jesus rather than the voice of Satan, the world, or one's flesh. According to Smith, discernment is "a discriminating choice between two or more competing options. It is an act of judgment."[11] In spiritual discernment, it is a choice between two goods. To choose evil is not an option. Smith expounds, "Discernment is a discriminating choice between two or more good options. . . . Good or evil is not the question; rather, the challenge is to know what is best."[12] *It is a matter of choosing the better of two options.* So in choosing a church planter it is a matter of choosing the best person for planting and not judging a person evil or unfit.

This decision must also be made in a spirit of humility. It is important to realize that God is God and people are not God. Humility, according to Ignatius Loyola, is "seeing oneself in truth."[13] God is holy, just, omniscient, and omnipotent, and people are not. *This humility is a necessary trait of the leadership team during the decision-making process.*

The selection decision should also be made in a time of consolation as opposed to a time of desolation. Consolation is "any feeling of peace, joy, contentment, or serenity. It is a sense of well-being, of all-rightness."[14] A jail pastor should not be chosen during a time of church conflict. This decision should not be made when the church or a member of the leadership team is going through a time of desolation. Desolation is "any feeling of anger, depression, discouragement or inner turmoil. Sometimes it may be a feeling of malaise, not a specific feeling or reaction, just inner discomfort or dis-ease."[15] If a member of the leadership team is experiencing desolation, he or she should be excused from the process. *There are many important church decisions that are made during desolation as opposed to consolation, which is why many churches make decisions they soon regret.*

In this discernment process, "Holy Scripture is the starting point and measuring rod for individual [and group] insight."[16] If the leadership wants to hear the voice of Jesus, then every member must be in God's Word. They each must be in Bible study and the daily reading of God's Word. Again, many bad decisions have been made in the Church by people who are not in God's Word. This is the only way to arrive at the truth regarding the correct choice and also eliminate evil as an option. Smith contends, "The Spirit will never contradict Scripture. When we are faced with competing options, both or all of which may be good and valid options, what we will long for is communion with Christ by His Spirit. So if we have neglected the study of Scripture, we will be at a distinct disadvantage."[17] God keeps his Word. *The leadership team needs to keep his Word in them.*

Prayer is also necessary during the selection process. *The type of prayer the leadership team needs to employ, however, is listening prayer.* Smith declares, "[Prayer] needs to be listening prayer. For so many, prayer is talking to God rather than communion with God. . . . Discerning prayer requires that at times we simply shut up and remain silent in the presence of God."[18] Too often believers are too busy telling God what should transpire rather than being inspired by the Holy Spirit. The intercessors will be praying for the discernment of the leadership team but the leadership team must plan on listening to God. This process takes time and cannot be rushed. God will provide the planter.

This discernment process must take place in the community of faith. No one person can discern apart from God's people, the body of Christ. Smith explains, "To be discerning people we need to know what it means to be in spiritual communion with fellow members of the body of Christ. We should know what it is to live in submission of the community, but particularly to those in appointed leadership within the church."[19] This means regular worship attendance as well as small group participation for every member of the leadership team. It is dangerous to the discernment process to simply assume every member of the team is worshipping and participating in a small group. The greater community can also have valuable input to the decision-making process. The discerning of jail pastors is not a covert activity. Smith states,

> We never discern in isolation; we discern in community. Every significant choice we make reflects the fact that we are profoundly interconnected with the lives of others. Our decisions inevitably affect others but are also affected by the choices that others make. It is only appropriate that we are accountable to others in our choices; others need to be able to challenge us and confirm whether what we believe to be God's will is truly of God. We need the wisdom and counsel of others.[20]

The leadership team does not need to fear input from other parts of the congregation. It is an important part of spiritual discernment.

This discernment process involves the groups' emotions as well as reason. Smith explains,

> God does not have a mouth; He does not speak audibly. Rather, God speaks to us through our feelings, impressions left on our minds. But we must not equate the voice in our head with the voice of God. We rather discern God's word in the interpretation of these impressions. We discern by perceiving and evaluating the movements of the heart. In the end it will be reason that guides us—but reason comes to

terms with the feelings and impressions that are left on our inner person.[21]

The leadership team will use its reason and emotions. Emotions are not something to fear but a means of listening to God. Emotions are to be embraced. *The group will function with reason but also listen to their instinctual gut feelings, as this is one way that God speaks.* This discernment process should also take place communally. Smith states, "The focus here is not on the prerogatives of the designated leaders or on the equal privileges of the members, but on the corporate responsibility for discerning the wisdom and prompting of the Holy Spirit."[22] The pastor (or any other leader) does not have any special input in the decision-making process. *The goal is for the group to hear Jesus' voice and make a correct judgment.* With this in mind, it is often true that there are people who are more gifted in discernment than others. They are more intuitive by nature. On Amazing Grace's church council, Robyn and Lydia are two women with a gift of discernment. The council weighs a decision heavily if one of these two sisters in Christ has a bad feeling about a council decision. In the same way, the leadership team will measure Lydia's and Robyn's input regarding future church planters.

During this jail planter selection process, the leadership team will also employ Spitale's requirements for ministry to the incarcerated. Spitale declares, "There are only four requirements for effective prison [jail] ministry: be yourself; speak the truth with compassion; love inmates and correctional officers with the love of Christ; live under the influence of the Holy Spirit and the Word of God."[23] In addition, the one qualification the leadership team absolutely requires of jail pastors is to know and love Jesus as stated by Henri Nouwen:

The question is not: How many people take you seriously? How much are you going to accomplish? Can you show some results? But: Are you in love with Jesus? Perhaps another way of putting the question would be: Do you know the incarnate God? In our world of lowliness and despair, there is an enormous need for men and women who know the heart of God, a heart that forgives, cares, reaches out and wants to heal. In that heart there is no suspicion, no vindictiveness, no resentment, and not a tinge of hatred. It is a heart that only wants to give love and receive love in response. It is a heart that suffers immensely because it sees the magnitude of human pain and the great resistance to trusting the heart of God who wants to offer consolation and hope.[24]

These are the types of people needed to plant churches in the darkness of the Maricopa County jails. Without this intimate knowledge and deep love of Christ, the jail pastors will not last in this mission field.

The selection team at Amazing Grace has already learned this lesson the hard way. One of the new jail churches was to have Jaime Gomez, a young Latino man, as a Spanish-speaking jail pastor and planter. The selection team went through the discernment process and decided Jaime was up to the mission. After the first worship service at Durango jail, Jaime left the ministry and the church. The thought of ministering to forty Latino men in chains and black and white stripes was simply too much for him. Although Jaime knows and loves Jesus, he did not have the depth of knowledge of Jesus and the depth of the love of Jesus necessary to plant a jail church. He could not withstand the onslaught of Satan. Jail church planters, and all church planters, need to have the heart of Christ first and foremost.

Initiating the Process for Jail Church Commencement

The first step for starting a jail church in the Maricopa County jail complex begins by the team leader contacting Head Chaplain Gregory Millard. The chaplain will then give the necessary paperwork to be filled out to the team leader and parent church pastor and distribute the information to the local jail chaplains. Because Amazing Grace knows the local chaplains intimately, however, Head Chaplain Millard is comfortable with the church directly working with the local jail chaplains. The local jail chaplains will then contact the team leader with the available time periods for worship. The team leader and church planter will decide which jail and which time is best for the new jail church.

In the past year, Amazing Grace has planted two new churches (one in Spanish and one in English) in the Durango jail, a men's facility. A third church in this jail was planted by the end of 2008. In this setting, the team leader will be working directly with Chaplain.

The jail pastors selected for these three Durango jail churches, after the process of communal spiritual discernment by the team, are Bryant Walton and Paul Scott. Bryant's wife Prisca will also be trained to assist Lydia and Cecilia at the women's facility, Estrella jail. Bryant and Prisca Walton are not members of Amazing Grace but feel called to minister in the jails. The leadership team has affirmed their call to the jail churches. The Holy Spirit cannot be limited to the members of Amazing Grace exclusively, which has been a point of learning by the leadership team.

It is necessary for the jail pastors to keep accurate attendance records for the sheriff. The parent church will be advised of these figures on a monthly basis. All jail pastors are required by the sheriff to have background checks, have a letter of reference from the parent church, be fingerprinted, and attend a three-hour class on the rules and safeguards in the jail complexes. Upon successful completion of training, the jail pastors receive badges with access to all jail complexes. Thereafter, once a year the pastors will be required to attend a one-hour class about procedures and updates for the jail complexes.

There are no direct costs to the jail churches. The parent church needs to include the jail churches in its annual budget. Figure 2 delineates the immediate and necessary financial needs for a jail church startup.

Figure 2. Financial Needs for a Jail Church Startup

- Gospel of John videos ($44)
- Gospel of Matthew DVD ($14)
- Fingerprints, background check, jail classes (no charge)
- Clear book bags ($14)
- Chalice, wafers ($7)
- Grape juice ($1, jail pastors' responsibility)
- Note cards and pencils ($7)

- Music CD ($10)
- Overhead transparencies ($5)
- 500 business cards ($36, first box purchased by the parent church)

The financial expenses will be paid for by the parent church other than where noted as the jail pastor's responsibility. The maximum cost for a church startup in the jails is approximately $138, plus $10 monthly to replenish supplies including note cards, pencils, and wafers.

The goals necessary to fulfill the vision are threefold. The first is to establish jail churches throughout the Maricopa County jail complex. The second is to have inmates worship at Amazing Grace or another Christian church upon release. And the third goal is to start churches outside the jail system planted by former inmates.

Amazing Grace's immediate steps are also threefold. First, the church will continue planting the three new jail churches. Second, leaders will coach/mentor the new jail pastors. Third, the jail pastors will coach/mentor certain inmates.

Amazing Grace's milestones include: 1) successfully birthing three new jail churches in 2008; 2) holding monthly jail pastors' meetings for debriefing and support; 3) having grandchildren jail churches start up in 2009; and 4) having great-grandchildren churches start outside of the jails by 2011. Before Amazing Grace launches the missions, the following steps will need to be taken: 1) prayer cover must be provided; 2) jail pastors must receive badges; 3) the time and place of churches must be negotiated with the chaplains; and 4) the jail pastors must be resourced, trained, mentored, and coached.

Amazing Grace plans to plant more than a dozen churches inside the jail complexes. The jail pastors, to start, will come from the parent church or other Christian churches. Eventually, released inmates will be the future church planters inside and outside the jails. As inmates are released who do not live near Amazing Grace, they will attend churches in their neighborhoods or start to plant churches in their neighborhoods. The concept is to empower inmates to plant churches not only in the jails, but to also become mission-aries for people living outside of the jails in their local neighbor-hoods. Logan explains, "Leadership training starts in the harvest."[25] Jesus used hands-on training, a kind of teaching that is paired with experience. It is also called it "show-how" training. Logan outlines this training: "I do, you watch; I do, you help; you do, I help; you do, I watch; you do, someone else watches."[26] This is the training format employed by Amazing Grace in training jail pastors and it has been tremendously effective. This model is also being employed by the jail pastors and inmates. The inmates also unconsciously use this model with other inmates. Like a snow ball rolling down a hill, the leadership continually grows.

Inspirational Worship

In the worship at the jails, the goal is to have the inmates meet Jesus and then be changed by Him. The jail ministers and volunteers of Amazing Grace want the inmates to be empowered to take Jesus back to their pods with them. Beckner and Park affirm this goal:

> What seems to work in church won't necessarily work in jails and prisons. The majority of prison ministries still use the church model of ministry, meaning either preaching services or Sunday school type Bible studies. . . . What is far more needed in prisons is systematic, foundational teaching with personal modeling, relationship building, and accountability.[27]

Hopefully some of the inmates will start to be changed inwardly and outwardly. Conversion and radical change is the goal. The goal is for the inmates to come to faith in Christ and become new creations. They are to start the journey of discipleship. Logan and Cole clarify, "The goal is not to start a church service, but to build a community of disciples."[28] This means the jail churches will have to be immersed in prayer.[29] The jail church worship service is an evolving process, but the components presently being used are listed in Figure 3.

Figure 3. Components of a Jail Church Worship Service

- Music-singing with CDs (or guitar when available) and an overhead projector
- Prayer request written on note cards and later distributed to the members of the parent church
- An order of confession
- Video Bible
- Bible reading
- Evangelistic preaching or witness talks
- Holy Communion
- Altar call in the form of a prayer
- Questions and answers
- Laying on of hands

The churches in the jails meet once a week at the location and time agreed upon with the chaplains. The jail chapel at Durango holds approximately fifty inmates but there will rarely be that many due to many detention officers' reluctance to bring in that many inmates. The jail pastor starts by shaking every inmate's hand. *(Use of hand sanitizer is mandatory.)* Then the pastor and inmates sing praises, fill out prayer cards, confess, pray, hear God's Word, and receive the Lord's Supper. The Lord's Supper is open to all and all are encouraged to receive. Baptisms are arranged with the chaplain and re-baptism does occur. Amazing Grace prefers to have the inmates baptized when released if they are not going to prison so they can become part of a church outside the jail complex. Where the inmates go upon release is just as important as their conversion inside the jails.

The dynamic in worship is the Holy Spirit. The jail pastor and inmates become one body in Christ and they can affect an entire pod of prisoners. They become brothers or sisters in Christ. The jail pastors set the tone for worship. A conversational tone in worship and casual dress is recommended. Inmates do not like clerical collars or robes. The jail pastors must be open and honest with the inmates but still set clear boundaries. They must also decide who can help them with worship. Audio, visual and participatory elements are all incorporated in worship. Sometimes spontaneous dance is even included in a very limited way. Anointing with oil has been employed at some jail churches, but the use of incense is prohibited. Amazing Grace's jail worship is extremely casual and the old Gospel hymns with a country sound are by far the favorite, although some contemporary or traditional hymns are used as well. "One Day at a Time" is the all-time favorite in both the English-language churches and the Spanish-language church. Depending on who is present, a Spanish song may be sung in an English-language church or vice versa.

The worship is a blended type of worship that is lay led. Creativity is lifted up with the inmates singing solos or playing the piano. The jail pastors are not necessarily gifted as worship leaders, but they have sincere and authentic hearts for worship. Their vulnerability in singing encourages the inmates to sing louder. *The worship at the jail churches is not a performance but is very heartfelt praise. It is a holy time that changes those involved.*

The fact that inmates are invited to Amazing Grace upon their release is very important. Inmates have broken down in tears when they were invited to worship at the mother church. Some believers volunteering in the jails might not encourage the inmates to attend their home church after release. All of Amazing Grace's jail pastors have business cards with maps to the church on the back and they distribute them freely.

Timeline for Implementation

The first two jail churches were planted in the Lower Buckeye jail, a men's facility, in the spring of 2006. Two additional jail churches were added in the Estrella jail, a facility for women, in the fall of 2007. Unfortunately at this time, Widney discontinued serving one jail church at Lower Buckeye because it was physically too demanding on him. Hence, Amazing Grace had three jail churches at the end of 2007.

In January of 2008, Amazing Grace started a Spanish-language jail church in the Durango jail led by Jaime Gomez. However, as mentioned above, this leadership position was too difficult for Jaime and he stepped down after the first meeting. During this time I, the senior pastor of the mother church, felt called to take Jaime's place as the jail pastor of the Spanish-language jail church. *Despite my imperfect Spanish, this jail church has flourished averaging forty inmates and once again I find myself humbled and blessed. The Holy Spirit empowers me and obviously gives the inmates the gift of ears.* Shortly after the Spanish-language jail church started, Amazing Grace planted another jail church (English-language) in Durango with jail pastors Paul Scott and Bryant Walton. At the same time, Prisca Walton became a jail pastor to help Lydia and Cecilia in the Estrella jail. By the end of 2008, there will be another jail church planted in Durango jail or Towers jail giving Amazing Grace a total of six jail churches in 2008. The leadership team and intercessors are currently praying for more jail pastors.

In 2009, Amazing Grace will plant at least another three jail churches followed by another three jail churches in 2010. In 2010, there should be some released inmates becoming jail church planters/pastors. There should also be a released inmate serving as the team leader. In 2011, Amazing Grace should plant its first church outside of the jails with a released inmate as the pastor in training. Needless to say, the Holy Spirit is moving in a very powerful way at Amazing Grace.

Multiplication of Churches and the Conversion/ Renewal of Inmates

At this point, the focus of Amazing Grace jail ministry is primarily on the church plants in the jails. The small groups meet in the pods after the church has worshipped at the various jail complexes. It is a rather unique situation for a church in that the jail pastors can only disciple, model, coach, and encourage the small groups while they are assembled en masse for corporate worship. The jail pastors rely on the Holy Spirit and the inmates to take the discipleship model back to the pods. Logan and Cole declare, "To multiply churches and groups without multiplying disciples is not only disobedient, but it is also nearly impossible!"[30] Church multiplication starts with making disciples and empowering people to learn by doing.

Modeling and walking with the person is of the utmost importance and the core of discipling.

The groups in the pods are groups of recovery, accountability, prayer, Bible study, evangelism and most importantly hope. The groups are prayer focused and Bible centered. They do not engage in the discipline of confession for legal purposes and physical safety. They meet in a variety of locations at many different times. The groups are lay led and the basic thrust is conversion, evangelism, discipleship, and hope. These groups start in the jails but upon release of the individual inmates, intense follow-up will be necessary by the mother church or the home congregation.[31] By God's grace, these ever-changing groups have multiplied and eventually will lead to new jail churches as well as eventual church plants outside the jail within a four-year period. These small rapidly multiplying groups, called *"hope groups,"* have an intimate relationship with Jesus and with one another. Logan and Cole describe the Amazing Grace jail hope groups when they state, "Because they have evangelism, spiritual formation and multiplication in their genetic code, the cell groups are far more likely to be healthy, growing and reproducing."[32] The hope groups have the right DNA because it has been passed on by the mother church and because they are experiencing the growth provided by the Holy Spirit.

The process of incorporating new inmates begins by their attending a jail church worship service. There the jail pastors will emphasize conversion and evangelism, which will be taken back into the pods. The jail pastors have discovered that most inmates actually come to corporate worship due to the small groups' effectiveness in the pods. They evangelize and invite continually in the small hope groups in the pods. With an ever-changing jail population, disciples will be raised up to teach and preach in the pods. The hope groups in the pods will always be changing and evolving. Upon release, these inmates will be an invaluable source of information and power for the parent church or other churches outside of the jails. Many inmates have already stated their desires to return to the jails to be jail pastors.

The jail churches primarily offer a center of hope, love, and power. The corporate meetings act as a battery to keep the small groups up and running. In the jail churches and the hope groups, authentic loving relationships help people to take the next step in their faith. Relationships develop such as mentor with student, coach with disciple, disciple with disciple, and back to mentor with student. Many of these relationships happen underground in the pods where the jail pastors really have no control. These relationships need to be loving, flexible, trustful, hopeful, empowering, and self-multiplying. This can be limited to some extent due to the context. *Meanwhile, back in the pods the hope groups are generally healthy, brutally honest, and as open as possible under these conditions. They usually do not share the dysfunctional patterns found in many churches.* Figure 4 depicts the ministry flow chart of the jail churches.

Figure 4. The Ministry Flow Chart of the Jail Churches

- Target ministry is corporate jail worship.
- Participate in hope group in the pods.
- Baptism can precede/follow any of the above.
- Modeling and discipling in large group and in hope groups.
- Empowered to serve.
- Eventual leadership in some capacity.
- Upon release, attend parent church or another Christian church.
- If they attend parent church, then they will attend Cursillo and/or Alpha.
- Possibly become a church planter in the jails or outside the jails.

The prototype group formed naturally at Lower Buckeye jail under the leadership of Widney and me. Kelly and Donald were both inmates at Lower Buckeye jail and attended the worship service. During worship, they both accepted Jesus as their Lord and Savior and both formed small hope groups in their pods. Eventually, Donald was moved to Towers jail where he started a Bible study for forty-five inmates. Meanwhile, Kelly was released on bond and has joined Amazing Grace. He attended Cursillo and then started a twelve-step group. Kelly, although currently serving time in prison, wants to become a jail pastor when the state allows him to do so. The strategy for inviting people to the hope groups involves their witnessing the change, conversion, and renewal in the inmates. The other inmates are desperate for hope and they see it incarnated in jail church members.

The willingness of the jail pastors to risk and love unconditionally is foundational in building relationships with the inmates and in their conversion and renewal. This has become contagious. Also important is authentic and inspirational worship. This does not mean the worship has to be fancy and the jail pastor has to be an accomplished worship leader. In fact, simple worship is best. Finally, the jail pastors must follow up with one-on-one visits when possible. Prayer, Bible study, Bible reading, and confession always need to be emphasized.

Upon release, the former inmates will become a part of a church. If they join Amazing Grace, they will hopefully attend Cursillo or Alpha. After the person has proven herself or himself to be a disciple, she or he may be considered in the discernment process to become a jail pastor. Widney or I will have one-on-one meetings with the prospective jail pastors and current jail pastors, and we will also meet once a month with all the jail pastors. I will make use of CoachNet,[33] an online resource center established by Logan, and other available resources. CoachNet will be a valuable tool to be placed in the hands of church planters and their coaches.

Furthermore, a coaching and/or mentoring relationship should be provided for the jail church planters as well as their coaches. For example, Pastor Gale Schmidt has served as my coach and mentor for both jail church planting and Spanish-language ministry for eight years. His experience and wisdom are of immeasurable worth. All church planters should have a coach and/or mentor relationship.

Amazing Grace is making disciples and is multiplying churches because it is an attractive and effective planting movement. Logan delineates the eight qualities of an attractive planting movement: reputation, vision, compassion for lost people, diversity, character, coaching, resources, and success.[34] These qualities are part of the jail church planting movement at Amazing Grace. It is important to note, additionally, that numerical growth does not define a successful ministry. The following letter, written by inmate Henri, defines the success of the home church's planting adventure:

Many say jailhouse conversions are a dime per dozen. I would bet that someone who would make a statement like that is not truly trusting fully in the Lord Jesus Christ. The way I see it, I would rather come to jail or prison once, twice, or however many times it takes and have my soul right with God, then to never come to jail or prison and be there on the streets on my way to hell. Amen? Praise God for what He is doing in prisons and jails everywhere. When asked, "Why do you wait until you get locked up to seek God?" My answer, "Because that is when I need Him most!!!"

Your last letter was a big blessing to me! I got goose bumps or as I like to call them "glory bumps" when I came to the end of it. It was a blessing to hear confirmation that the Lord is still at work in me, still using me, and still getting the glory in my life despite all the bad decisions. He is good at that . . . Amen?

In all successful planting movements, Henri is right when he writes, "God is still getting the glory." Henri agrees with Saint Paul who wrote, "Let him who boasts, boast in the Lord" (1 Cor. 1:31). In order for Henri and the other inmates to have a chance at life after they are released, however, there needs to be a connection between them and a mother church.

CHAPTER 6

CONNECTING THE MOTHER CHURCH AND THE JAIL CHURCHES

The Prayer Connection: Inside and Outside

Prayer is the glue that binds the jail churches with the mother church. Prayer is not simply an addition to the process. It holds the process together. It is the most powerful weapon the Church can employ against the adversary. Logan and Cole explain, "When you engage in the business of building the Church, you engage in spiritual warfare; they go together."[1] Make no mistake, to enter into jail ministry is to enter into the deadliest kind of spiritual warfare. The Church is attacking one of Satan's strongholds, the jails. E.M. Bounds has said, "Prayer is not preparation for the battle, prayer is the battle."[2] This spiritual battle takes place primarily on two fronts: outside the jails in the prayers of the mother church, and inside the jails in the prayers of the jail churches.

The prayer cover, intercession, for the battle of the jail churches started on the outside with the prayers of the mother church. This prayer cover began in 2006 with the prayer chain consisting of about forty people and the daily prayer ministry consisting of approximately fifty people (implementation of these ministries was discussed in Chapter 5.) In addition, in 2008 Amazing Grace began a Monday evening prayer meeting consisting of another twenty intercessors. Occasionally, these prayer warriors will do prayer walks around the church grounds or neighborhood. *These brothers and sisters who pray on Monday evenings are the prayer special forces of Amazing Grace.* Since initiating this service the Spirit has been unleashed at Amazing Grace, changing and spiritually growing the membership and the ministries. More importantly it has paved the way for the new jail churches.

The main connection between the mother church and the jail churches is the prayer request cards written by the inmates. At the beginning of each jail service, note cards and pencils are distributed to the inmates. The inmates write their names and prayer requests on the cards. The requests consist of prayers for their wives, girl-friends, children, grandchildren, parents, and court appearances. As the inmates mature, however, the prayer requests are for faith for themselves, the other inmates, their families, and others. They also often ask for prayer for their jail pastors. All of these prayer requests are then collected and prayed over by the jail pastors. The following Sunday at worship, they are distributed to the members of the mother church. The prayer requests are in both Spanish and English. The members take the cards home and pray daily for the inmates for one week and sometimes longer, depending on the member who receives them.

These prayer requests have formed a tremendous bond between the inmates and the mother church. These two very different groups of people come to know each other before the throne of God in prayer before they even or ever have a chance to meet. When the inmates are released and visit the mother church, they see the saints who have been upholding them in prayer. At the same time, the members see the saints they have been praying for behind jail bars. It is a very holy time. One memorable such meeting was the first time Amazing Grace member Hazel Spencer met former inmate Kelly Preiss at a Sunday service at Amazing Grace. The first thing Hazel said was, "Kelly, you are the one I have been praying for." These meetings are extremely joyous occasions.

Furthermore, both the inmates and members of the mother church experience the power of prayer. For example, there was a praise shared in Amazing Grace's Sunday worship by jail pastor Paul Scott. One inmate was facing a minimum of fourteen years in prison, and there was no way he could receive a more lenient sentence. After sending in numerous prayer requests to the mother church, however, this inmate received only six months' probation. Amazing Grace and this inmate witnessed the power of prayer first-hand. This type of praise report has become a common occurrence in the churches. The prayers outside the jails are a powerful spiritual force.

Inside the jails, the mother church and jail churches receive additional prayer cover. The jail pastors ask the inmates for prayer for personal prayer requests or prayer requests from the mother church. Logan describes the power of this vulnerability: "Intercession is a heavy burden. When leaders allow themselves to need the support of others and be cared for in prayer, they become a more connected part of the whole body of Christ."[3]

When the jail pastor returns the following week for worship, the inmates always ask for updates to the prayer requests. It makes the inmates feel connected and important to the body of Christ. *Their faith regarding prayer is fresh and childlike.* It is clear to all that the inmates' prayers are very powerful and effective. In response to their prayers, marriages have healed, cancer has been cured, and addicts have entered recovery. It is amazing that inmates locked in cages can focus on others outside the jails and pray for them and their churches. This is a very holy and profound experience.

Although prayer walks have been employed outside the jails at the mother church, there is still a need to do prayer walks at the jail complexes. Logan and Cole write, "Prayer walking creates intentional opportunities to walk and pray through specific communities where new churches will be planted with an eye for specific needs, opportunities, and insights. This approach can be modified to pray for whole districts and regions."[4] Most likely these prayer walks will take place in the jail parking lots due to the jail's security policies within the complex.

The Jail Pastors' Connection

The jail pastors are the beginning of the relationship between the inmates and the church outside of the jails. Therefore, it is critical that the jail pastors reflect the love of Christ to the inmates. Logan and Cole declare, "People must see God in us."[5] By reflecting the love of God, the jail pastors can demonstrate and create a Christian community in the jails. One of the main points the jail pastors emphasize is that the Church is people. Therefore, when the inmates meet together for study or worship, they are the Church. *The inmates need to realize they are the body of Christ. They are God's people.* Logan and Cole clarify, "Made in His image, the church is meant to be a community, which can simply be defined as a shared life. Koinonia, a Greek word meaning Christian fellowship with others, is the New Testament framework that forms a partnership in mission."[6] Hence, when they are released the inmates will seek another body of believers to have fellowship with. This may or may not be the mother church. The choice of church is not important; what is important is that the inmates remain in Christian community outside the jails. In my experience as a jail pastor and urban pastor, the first step in a released inmate's return to jail or prison is cessation of worship attendance. *When the person stops coming to worship they start returning to jail.*

The example of authenticity and love the jail pastor demonstrates will determine how connected the inmates become with one another at the jail church. It also determines how connected the inmates will be with a church after release. Because discipleship is caught more than taught, jail pastors must understand how very important their presence is to the inmates. Spitale shares,

I met one inmate at Florida State Prison, an unbeliever at the time, who observed: "You know when you Christians come on the block, the place seems to get lighter. I can almost see the darkness retreating down the tier as you approach." Others have said, "It doesn't seem so depressing when you folks are here." Never underestimate the value of your presence in the lives of inmates, whether you are confined in the chapel or permitted on the tiers. They genuinely look forward to your arrival.[7]

The jail pastors or planters may be the first glimpse of Christ some inmates have ever seen. Unfortunately, this may be the first peek they have of what the Church is supposed to be.

This is why such great care needs to be taken in choosing a jail church planter. It is necessary that the jail planters comprehend the fact that they have been commissioned by Christ as his ambassadors into the darkness of the jails. They are the incarnation of God's love to the inmates. Covert expounds,

> Even so Christ the healer sends us. He sends us to the unnatural thing, to be in contact with evil, to be involved with sickness and suffering. He commends us to heal. He knows that we require a commission, and he gives it. We do not only love, but we are sent to love. . . .Only those who believe that they have been sent by God to do battle with evil will be able to drink the cup that he drank, and to give as they have received [8]

The jail church pastors, although laity, are in the front lines of the battle in the fight for the souls of the inmates. The jail pastors establish or reestablish a relationship with Christ and his Church that will carry on outside the jails. These lay pastors serve as a bridge between two worlds (or two kingdoms) for the inmates.

Preaching in the Jails and the Mother Church

The preaching in the jails is straightforward biblical preaching. The gospel message is the focus of every lesson, and the jail pastor always reads directly from the Bible. Covert explains, "The Bible is always best, especially in settings where there is a high turnover of inmates, such as a county jail. You want to demonstrate visibly where you get your information and what you rely on as authoritative truth."[9] *Unlike our secular culture, the inmates trust the Bible as authoritative even though they probably do not trust Christians.*

Therefore, Scripture is emphasized in worship and recommended for study in the small groups meeting in the pods.

The preaching is not fancy but hard-hitting evangelistic preaching that challenges the inmates to make a choice for Jesus. The inmates have tried many things that the world offers and find themselves in the county jail, which they refer to as a "hell hole." Surprisingly, many inmates do not even know the foundational Bible stories or who Jesus is. Spitale declares, "Many young people coming into prison today have never heard that Jesus died on a cross for their sins. This may sound incredible to many, but it is the truth. Even in the case of many African Americans, who have long been the beneficiaries of a rich, Christian heritage in our country, the old assumptions can no longer be made."[10] The preaching must be the basic Christian message that Jesus alone is the answer to the problems of sin, death, and the devil. The message must be Christocentric. Many churches outside the jail complex could also heed these words.

In addition, the inmates' lives are broken and they know it. The preaching in the jails must address this brokenness with the wholeness only Christ can provide. This message is necessary both inside and outside the jails. Van Gelder states,

> Within the living communities of faith, we need to concentrate on developing a message of wholeness and healing to a postmodern world characterized by fragmentation and brokenness. This message will need to be directed to both the church and the world [the jails]. Our church practices can no longer assume that Christian people have their lives together. In our ministries we will need to develop more capacity to allow people to engage in a process of experiencing healing and living lives of holistic discipleship.[11]

My experience as a jail pastor and an urban pastor for the past twelve years affirms Hunsberger and Van Gelder's statement. Most of the people entering the urban church are broken. The only difference between them and the inmates is that the inmates know their lives are broken. Wholeness and healing need to be preached in the mother church, as well as in the jail churches.

The most important message to be preached in the mother church is acceptance of all people through the love of Christ and evangelism. Hence, Amazing Grace's mission statement to love all people to Christ must be lifted up at every opportunity. The congregation continually needs to be reminded and encouraged to love all people, including inmates and their families. One of the continual themes in the Gospels is Jesus reaching out to society's outcasts. If this was a continual theme for Jesus then it needs to be a continual theme for believers today, his disciples. Fischer illustrates this point:

> That means I can look and listen for what is noble and admirable in everyone around me: everyone, even the unseemly, such as non-Christians, nerds, political enemies, murderers, fascists, and the profane. We look across at eye level to everyone. Something can be found even in the fallen. There is no place we can relegate the scumbags of the world. Only God can do that. Our responsibility is to look for what is redeemable.[12]

There is no place for pharisaical attitudes in a church reaching out into the jails. In fact, there should not be a pharisaical attitude in any church that bears the name of Christ. Unfortunately, Amazing Grace has received families of inmates who had been marginalized in other Christian churches. This is a travesty.

Another message that must be preached in the mother church as well as the jail churches is the opportunity to accept Jesus Christ as Lord and Savior. There are nominal Christians outside the jails as well as inside the jails. Some type of altar call needs to be consistently offered in the mother church. The emphasis is commitment to Christ and life change. Clapp explains, "Evangelism in a non-Constantinian setting [where the church is no longer the center of culture] requires that evangelism be understood not simply as declaring a message to someone but as an invitation into the world-changing kingdom of God."[13] The members of the mother church and jail churches are to understand that discipleship, being a Christian, involves entering into the kingdom of God and a completely different paradigm than what the world offers. It is more than worshipping one Sunday a month and throwing loose change into the plate. It is a gradual and complete life transformation. The inmates need to hear this and so do the members of the local church. Jesus says in the Book of Revelation, "These are the words of the Amen, the faithful and true witness, the ruler of God's creation. I know your deeds, that you are neither cold nor hot. I wish you were either one or the other! So, because you are lukewarm—neither hot nor cold—I am about to spit you out of my mouth" (Rev. 3:14-17). Christians, incarcerated or free, are not to be lukewarm. Unfortunately, there are many people today who do not want to hear about the cost of discipleship. In some cases people have left Amazing Grace due to the challenge of transformation in a sermon or a bible study. *Although painful for the pastor, the truth is there are many lukewarm churches these people can choose to attend.*

Welcome into the Mother Church

It does not matter how effective a jail church is in evangelism and discipleship if the inmates, like Henri, are not welcomed into a local church upon their release from prison or jail. Beckner and Park state,

> Offenders, who have been released from jail or prison, need to become caring members of the community. The church as an accepting community, can facilitate reintegration for both the offender and the victim. The secular community does not always address these issues, but the Christian community is commanded to reach out to the isolated and ostracized. The Church is the critical component of the restorative justice ministry paradigm.[14]

The Church needs to start being the body of Christ and welcome tax collectors, sinners, and released inmates and their families. This means the local congregation must make changes and take risks. This is extremely difficult for many congregations. After all, change and risk are not on accepted terms in the greater Church. It is precisely by changing and taking risks, however, that the Church finds life. Logan declares, "If a church ever loses that edge of taking risks, they are going to become a church that needs to be revitalized. Taking risks keeps churches alive."[15] As a testimony to the truth of this statement, Amazing Graze has blossomed physically and spiritually by risking the adventure of welcoming the outcasts.[16]

The risk is worth it because ultimately it can save a lost soul. The inmates have experienced Christ in the jail churches and the pods. They have started the journey of discipleship and have experienced eternal life. The local church must enfold these new Christians under its wings so they can survive the onslaughts of the devil. Beckner and Park affirm this point: "When they [inmates] left the institution to return to their communities, I encouraged them to get involved in a local church. I knew that involvement in church upon release was vital to their survival as a Christian"[17] The newly released inmates, brothers and sisters in Christ, need the support of the local church.

Not only will the support of the local church keep these new Christians alive spiritually, but it can also keep these new Christians from returning to jail or prison. Beckner and Park indicate, "Research on the impact of religiosity [being part of a church] and crime is suggestive. Heavy participation in church attendance has been shown to have some impact on recidivism rates."[18] The recidivism rate is the number of inmates who return to jail or prison. Being part of a church community reduces recidivism. According to Schwarz, eighty percent is the normal recidivism rate of criminals.[19] The Church can help the former inmates start new lives and not return to the jails or prisons. *It is time for local churches to open their hearts and doors.*

The local congregation has to become a means of grace and love to newly released inmates. The model for the local church is Jesus. Saint Paul explains, "Each of you should look not only to your own interests, but also to the interests of others. Your attitude should be the same as that of Christ Jesus: Who, being in very nature God did not consider equality with God something to be grasped, but made himself nothing, taking the very nature of a servant" (Phil. 2:4-6). Covert clarifies,

Based on these truths, it is important that the church project a presence that draws people to God's fellowship where divine grace is dispensed in transforming and sustaining ways. The church should be experiential, touching the lives of others concretely. As the embodiment of Christ, the church should reflect a sacrificial and practical servanthood whose healing elements bring comfort and hope. Like the ministry of the Good Samaritan, the priesthood should not be afraid to reach out to those who are different and walk in their misfortune. This ministry of faith should accept God's call to the undesirable, the morally diseased, and the forgotten segments of society. In essence, Christian ministry must be a visible and involved conscience that is patterned after the life of Christ in order to bring healing and life to the sick and those who are motivated by evil.[20]

This attitude should flow from a Christian's heart. If the local congregation cannot embrace the formerly incarcerated, then there is a spiritual problem in the church that must be addressed. *To help these people is not optional but a command of Christ.* In the parable of the sheep and the goats, Jesus tells the goats (those who did not obey him), "I was a stranger and you did not invite me in, I needed clothes you did not clothe me, I was sick and in prison and you did not look after me" (Matt. 25:43).

In welcoming inmates the church needs to provide programs to assist in their rehabilitation. The local church cannot provide all the services but it can provide information regarding agencies that can help. Covert explains,

There is nothing more important for released prisoners than aftercare; after all, these individuals seldom have the resources to become stable citizens on their own. They need assistance that begins while they are still incarcerated. In other words, networking prior to release is necessary to prevent inmates from being overwhelmed by the new challenges of freedom, whether they receive support from a local church, a counseling agency, a therapeutic center, a workshop, or a job training program. Many individuals and organizations can assist returning felons but only through community awareness and inmate networking.[21]

Amazing Grace provides English as a Second Language (ESL) classes, a food pantry, a community service program, and a state-approved Christian daycare, all of which serve families of inmates and inmates themselves upon release. Amazing Grace also distributes a folder (put together by a former inmate) with information regarding government agencies to assist the former inmates. Offering community service opportunities is a very easy and very beneficial program any church can begin. It is a matter of getting registered with the probation department and supervising work projects for the local congregation. Amazing Grace uses people on probation for janitorial services, yard cleaning, kitchen help, and to help with its rummage sale. This program helps both the former inmates and the local church.

There are obstacles to becoming a welcoming place for the formerly incarcerated. Foremost is the reluctance of churches to accept released inmates as brothers and sisters in Christ. Shaw explains, "The churches are not only not interested in what goes on behind prison [jail] walls, but have, as well very little interest in accepting ex-offenders into their midst."[22] *This is a spiritual problem. It is sin and the Church must repent of its reluctance to love the released inmates and incarcerated.* Shaw declares, "Oh, they'll donate money, erect statues, give Bibles and greeting cards, and offer prayers for the lost souls, but they rarely get personally involved in Angola (a prison). Instead, they keep their involvement at a distance and feed its imprisoned souls with a long handled spoon."[23] The local church has to get involved with this ministry that it has abdicated to the states and to parachurch organizations. Jesus never kept his distance from lepers, the blind, the lame, the unclean, prostitutes, or sinners. In fact, he labeled his adversaries hypocrites for neglecting these people. It is time to swing wide the doors of the Church.

Another obstacle many inmates face when entering the Church upon their release is their personal history with the Church. Many inmates have been mistreated and even brutalized by the Church in the past. Shaw describes an example of church abuse:

> Another inmate remembered wandering into a church as a child and being thrown out by an usher who told him, "Get out, this is no place for loafers." When in tears he later told his mother of this incident at home she comforted him in words appropriate to their station in life. "The likes of you don't belong there," she said. "Church is only for nice people." . . . The inmate confessed, "I guess I'm still not nice people."[24]

Getting over this type of experience is difficult. Inmates are haunted with this past rejection even though the local church may be open to receiving them. At Amazing Grace, inmates are always wary when they visit for the first time. They do not know how people will react to them after they know their stories. Fortunately, usually after the first visit their minds are set at ease. They find that many of the people in the congregation were praying for them while they were incarcerated. In fact, the members of the church are happy when they match a name with a face.

The authority of the Church in the world is also a barrier the inmates have to overcome. Covert explains,

> Church authority is another stumbling block for some offenders. A significant number of convicted criminals detest authority of any kind, and this attitude carries over to the church. Authority problems resist easy solutions. In the majority of cases prisoners react to authority with unconscious responses that have been nurtured over the years. As such, the church can only build trust through a progressive and consistently compassionate presence.[25]

Although the trouble with authority is the personal issue of the inmate or released person, it is still an obstacle. This authority image must be overcome in the jail churches and in the mother church. In the jails, the jail pastors do not wear clerical collars or robes and strive to be as down to earth as possible. This helps, but the jail pastors have the advantage of more than one opportunity to reach the inmates. The mother church has one visit during which to ease their minds. A warm welcome is a necessity for a newly released person.

The formerly incarcerated have to struggle with the perception that they are not perfect but that everyone else in the church is seemingly without flaws. Spitale elucidates, "The temptation to return to this old [criminal] society can be especially strong if they continue to feel awkward and uncomfortable in their new, outside Christian experience. Often their initial impression of Christians in churches on the outside is that they all seem to have their acts together. It tends to make them feel very much out of place."[26] This obstacle can be overcome if the members of the mother church can be genuine. The church must be open and honest about its brokenness and imperfections. The inmates can tell if the church is being authentic or putting on airs of righteousness. They have literally lived in a world of con artists. Fischer contends,

> If the whole point of the Gospel is the forgiveness of sins, then why do we insist on continually parading these almost perfect lives in front of each other? How has it happened that the people who proclaim forgiveness of sin don't seem to have any sins to be forgiven them? How has the church that once was the happy possession of common fishermen and prostitutes and tax collectors become the home of the spiritually elite? There are, undoubtedly, numerous and complicated answers to these questions, but I believe at the root of them is lurking the issue of the Pharisee.[27]

Christians in the local church should be honest and vulnerable with one another. It is a very sad situation that the Church has become so dysfunctional that these words have to be written. If the Church can be authentic and non-Pharisaical, then former inmates and all visitors will feel welcome. The end and hoped for result is that demonstrated by the following letter by Cathy Gardner to Sheriff Arpaio:

Recently my son spent time in Lower buckeye jail. During that time he had the great fortune to attend "Jail Church," and meet Pastor Bezanson from Amazing Grace Christian Church. I believe the Lord led him to attend that service. My son is out on bail and faces prison time, but with the understanding and acceptance he got from members of this church he now has hope for a better future. We have together been attending services at Amazing Grace and finding continued hope for now and the future.

Please accept the heartfelt thanks of this mother, whose son was lost but is now found. By your provision of a meeting place and time for the Amazing Grace members to share the Word of God, it is possible for all who will listen to find the same hope and peace.[28]

Kindness and hospitality are part of the DNA of a healthy welcoming church. By God's grace, Amazing Grace possesses this genetic code. If the mother church does not have this DNA, then it is wise to get it right before entering any mission field.

Witness Talks: Inmates and Members of the Mother Church[29]

"Witness talks" and testimonies are regularly given in the jail churches by the jail pastors. These give the inmates hope in God's power to change lives, particularly for Jesus to change the inmate's life. Witness talks are also read aloud, listened to on CD or DVD, or occasionally given by a guest speaker. Beckner and Park attest to their effectiveness: "That's why it's important to put simple Christian witness and testimony books into prisons [jails]. When a prisoner can actually see someone's life change from bad to good, it creates hope deep inside his or her heart and soul. Then the Holy Spirit's allowed to come in and then you can look at the more serious Christian teaching."[30] When people give their testimonies in jail, this gives the inmates hope and also helps dispel the myth that Christians are perfect. The jail pastors' testimonies demonstrate that God usually uses things and people that are foolish according to earthly standards. Saint Paul declares, "But God chose the foolish things of the world to shame the wise; God chose the weak things of the world to shame the strong. He chose the lowly things of this world and the despised things—and the things that are not—to nullify the things that are, so that no one may boast before Him" (1 Cor. 1:27-29). Fischer illuminates this concept: "We continue to believe that God uses good people. We simply have a hard time finding drunks, cheats, liars, womanizers, adulterers, and murderers on God's Favorite People list."[31] *When the inmates embrace the fact that they are on God's favorite people list, then they experience freedom from their past and hope for their future.* Moreover, it empowers the inmates to believe God can use them.

And in fact God does use them, not only in the jails but through their prayer requests and upon their release into the local church. Amazing Grace has been blessed to have some of the released inmates become members. Graciously, they give their witness talks to the congregation and in so doing they encourage the membership in its faith. They teach the mother church how to be witnesses and disciples. Fischer describes what takes place when this occurs:

What the tax collector has to offer the Pharisee is what the poor always have to offer the rich: a clear sight of what is truly important in life. In this way the poor sinners are better than the rich and righteous. And Jesus was always on their side. If a Pharisee wants to recover, a good place to begin would be to look up to those she or he formerly would have judged. I have had the privilege on a few occasions to sing to Christian inmates in prison and be taught by them. To be in the presence of men and women behind bars who know God and experience true freedom is a humbling experience. I've never done this when I didn't wonder what side of the bars I was really on. It's a strange feeling to be dwarfed by the spirituality of prisoners and bound by the cares and the pleasures of the world that taunt me incessantly. They have so little of what the world offers but so much of God. I, in turn, have so much of what the world offers, and often experience so little of God. I have much to learn from these people.[32]

Amazing Grace has learned from the inmates while incarcerated and upon their release. The church has learned to be vulnerable and honest with one another. The members have learned the power of prayer and the power in confessing sin. The leaven of the inmates has helped Amazing Grace to become and remain healthy and has protected it from dysfunction. These are blessings that as a pastor I never expected to receive. It is awesome to see how wonderfully God works through his favorite people.

Cursillo Support and Recovery Groups

One part of the discipleship process at Amazing Grace is Lutheran Cursillo. Cursillo is a short course in Christianity that takes place on a three-day retreat weekend. Some of the equivalent movements to Lutheran Cursillo are Catholic Cursillo, Walk to Emmaus, Tres Dias, Via de Cristo, and Kairos. I have been involved in Cursillo in many ways, including as a spiritual director, for the past fifteen years. During this time, I have seen countless lives changed. Many people have taken the step from being a member of a church to becoming a disciple of Jesus Christ.

Kairos is a form of Cursillo employed in prisons, which Beckner and Park describe:

> Kairos is an outgrowth of the Christian renewal movement, called Cursillo (little course). The first in-prison version was led by Kairos founder Tom Johnson in Union Correctional Institution in Florida, in 1976. It is now active in 25 states, England and Australia, with ministry in 165 prisons and 13 outside groups for wives and mothers. More than 85,000 incarcerated men and women have been introduced to the Christian community of Kairos with over 20,000 volunteers having participated in 2,300 weekends around the world. . . . South Carolina studies of Kairos reveals that fewer by 10% of Kairos men and women return to prison within three years, a 28% improvement of the norm. And a recent study by the Florida DOC on Kairos participants at Union Correctional Institution reported a whopping 33% to 57% drop inmate recidivism rate.[33]

Kairos currently is prohibited in Arizona prisons. However, those released inmates who become members of Amazing Grace are encouraged to attend Cursillo. After their Cursillo retreat most inmates have grown in their faith and have become Jesus' disciples.

One released inmate was relapsing with crack cocaine. In fact he relapsed six times in a six-month period. Since his Cursillo retreat, the man has remained clean of drugs completely and he is now finishing his second year of sobriety. Meanwhile, this inmate has been a powerful witness for Christ and has led many people to Jesus. This man's success is due in large part to the small accountability groups that meet together regularly after the Cursillo retreat weekend.

These accountability groups are essential in the restoration of the relationship of the inmate with society. Each released inmate needs to be in relationship with a small group. Covert explains,

> Relationships influence success; therefore, in addition to structured support, released offenders need to have positive friendships that help them resist any circumstances that are detrimental to their welfare. In their weakened and susceptible state, even brief encounters with the wrong people could lead released felons back to prison. Church groups are increasingly becoming involved in outreach programs to prisoners and their families, and they have been a stabilizing force. Members of these groups are often instrumental in keeping felons engaged in constructive relationships and productive activities.[34]

The Cursillo small groups serve this purpose. Small group Bible studies, recovery groups, and prayer circles serve the same purpose. One Alcoholic Anonymous (AA) meeting at Amazing Grace aided a man named Bill, a Native American previously incarcerated, in his recovery and also led to his sobriety. Although Bill never became a member of Amazing Grace, he has maintained relationships with a few members and is in his second year of sobriety. Amazing Grace has learned that small groups, Cursillo or otherwise, are necessary for restoring inmates to wholeness.

The Ongoing Conversion/Renewal of Inmates

The conversion and renewal of inmates begin in the county jail but must continue in the local church. The released inmates need the community of faith to grow and to simply survive. Clapp insists, "Christian faith, far from being a manner solely between the individual and God, amounts to being grafted into a new people."[35] *The inmates need to be grafted into the local church or they will surely return to jail.* This is a message the jail pastors continually preach.

The inmates know they need Christian community and they expect to find it in the local church. Covert expounds,

> While imprisonment is an extreme hardship, it forces residents to reflect on the past and ponder the future. At this point the church frequently comes into focus. Many prisoners have Christian roots, and during their darkest hours these roots are remembered. Prison [jail] life leads individuals to look to the spiritual realm for solutions to their problems. They come to know the claims and promises of Jesus Christ and his church.[36]

The inmates know they need the Church to stay out of jail. They also have tasted Christ and want to continue to grow in him. This means becoming part of his Church outside of jail. It is only in the Church that the inmates will receive the nurture and modeling they need to grow into disciples. Logan's "show-how" model of training and discipleship (in which the steps are, as mentioned above: I do, you watch; I do, you help; you do, I help; you do, I watch: you do, someone else watches) cannot be implemented unless the inmates are grounded in a group of disciples.

Through this attachment the inmates will experience the Holy Spirit and transformation. The inmates desire a transformational experience. The Church needs to provide the environment for such an experience. Gibbs challenges the Church:

It demands a transforming experience of God and a deeper engagement with Scripture, both in fashioning the internal life of the church and defining its mission in the world. Churches will need to become genuinely apostolic congregations committed to living out their faith in the world, feeling comfortable operating on the frontlines and prepared to venture into new territory. They will need to recognize that without the sovereign activity of the Holy Spirit, people who are outside of Christ and immersed in a neo-pagan culture are "dead through the trespasses of sins . . . following the course of this world, following the ruler of the power of the air, the spirit that is now at work among those who are disobedient . . . following the desires of the flesh and senses" (Eph. 2:1-3). People who are spiritually dead are not aware of any needs until they are awakened by the persistent prompting of the Holy Spirit and the glimpses He gives of a more attractive alternative condition.[37]

The local church is to be a model of the more attractive alternative condition. This model is formed, sustained, and continually changed by the Holy Spirit. *The Church and individual Christians, including the inmates, are dependent on the Holy Spirit for transformation. A Spirit-filled community, a church, is required to continue discipling and transforming the members of the mother church and jail churches.* By God's grace Amazing Grace is a Spirit-filled and Spirit-led community.

CHAPTER 7

EVALUATION

The Process

The most important part of evaluating a jail church is *focusing on one's successes rather than one's failures*. Focusing on the failures would lead to complete frustration and depression. Schwarz explains:

> Do not measure the worth of jail and prison ministries by your failures. Measure its worth by your successes. You are part of a worldwide network that is changing the world—one jail and prison at a time, one person at a time. There are many challenges to jail and prison ministry, but there are also tremendous rewards. Volunteers often start working with inmates and ex-offenders thinking, I'll go into this dark place and take the love of God. Very often, they come out testifying, "I got more than I gave."[1]

At Amazing Grace, the jail pastors preach the gospel to approximately five thousand inmates each year. Since the jail ministry was launched in 2006, a handful of former inmates and their families have joined the church. Although they have had a tremendous impact on the mother church, the success of a jail ministry is believers' simple obedience to Jesus' command. Nevertheless, an evaluation process will be applied to the mother church and jail churches.

Evaluation of this strategy will be implemented through the use of two surveys. The questions in the first survey, found in Appendix B, were designed for members of the mother church to rate their spiritual condition before and after the establishment of the jail churches. Certainly this is not an exhaustive list of factors that could influence the members' spiritual condition. However, from the written comments on the surveys, it is clear that the planting of jail churches played a part in the members' spiritual growth. The survey was recently completed by sixty-three members of Amazing Grace. It is designed to measure: worship attendance; Bible study attendance; giving of time, talent, and treasure; practice of prayer; and the spirit of love.

The questions in the second survey, found in Appendix C, are identical to the latter section of church members' survey. This survey is completed by inmates after they have attended a jail church. The survey was recently completed by eighty-eight inmates. It is also designed to measure: worship attendance; Bible study attendance; giving of time, talent, and treasure; practice of prayer; and the spirit of love.

It is impossible to measure a person's spirituality. As Shaw comments regarding evaluation by different chaplains:

> As another chaplain noted: "Inmates are very good at letting you know." Other chaplains qualified this concept: "A good barometer," decided one, "is how many inmates come to talk and ask no favors." "I know I am doing a good job," said another, "when inmates communicate with me on a one to one basis for long-term counseling. This is happening as inmates consider me to be a teacher, a carer, a helper." . . . "If I am here it is," said one, adding, "success at best is a fleeting concept." Another wrote that "I would measure success by the amount of myself I put in to what I was doing, not on the number of people responding." A third decided that, from the vantage point of faith, the matter was ineffable. "There is no human evaluation form," he said. "I get a night's rest. God does the bookkeeping, if any is done."[2]

God does the bookkeeping. Believers are simply to plant seeds and the Lord of the harvest provides the growth. This survey, however, will attempt to grasp an insight of one's spirituality through one's spiritual practices.

The Members' Responses

When Amazing Grace planted jail churches, I expected Jesus to change the inmates who became part of the jail churches. I never thought, however, that the inmates in the jail churches would have such a wonderful impact on Amazing Grace. In response to the survey, sixty-six members of Amazing Grace (out of 135 members who have attended since 2006) rated themselves in worship, Bible study, giving, prayer, and love. They rated themselves in July 2008, first recalling the time before the jail churches started in 2006 and secondly responding with their current involvement.

Before 2006, 67 percent of respondents agreed or agreed strongly that their worship attendance was high. After 2006, 92 percent of respondents agreed or agreed strongly about their worship attendance. This is a net increase of 25 percent in personal worship practice. The members' responses in Figure 5 affirm these statistics.

Figure 5. Responses that reflect higher worship attendance

It has helped my son, and gotten him involved in church. —Jim

Brought me back to church. —Mike

My faith has increased and I have come to a whole new wonderful level of awareness. It is almost like I had been worshipping with my eyes shut. —Cathy

In fact, there have been a few people attending our church after they get out of jail. I think this is awesome! —Anonymous

It has also inspired the members of Amazing Grace to look at their own shortcomings. — Pastor Kopatz

It makes me feel comfortable enough to come and worship. — Chrissy

It has helped us to grow spiritually. — Darol

We've grown by leaps and bounds. — Ryan

These comments provide a glimpse of the excitement the jail churches have had on worship at Amazing Grace. In 2006, the average weekly worship attendance at Amazing Grace was 135 per week. In 2007, weekly attendance increased to 146 per week. In 2008, the average weekly attendance stands at 176 through July. Although the increase is not completely due to the jail churches, based on the members' responses it is part of the equation.

Before 2006, 44 percent of the respondents agreed or strongly agreed regarding their Bible study attendance. After 2006 the number of those who agreed or strongly agreed pertaining to Bible study rose to 62 percent. This is an 18 percent increase. The members of the mother church expound on this in Figure 6.

Figure 6. Responses that reflect higher Bible study attendance

It has also challenged us to look at our own relationship with Christ. — Pastor Kopatz

The jail ministry has made me more committed to the Lord than ever. — Cecilia

It helped me see how much further I need to grow. — Bryant

Willingness, a conscious and deliberate desire to serve and share the word of the Lord. — Cathy

The greatest increase in Bible study attendance has been the Wednesday night study on the Book of Acts. In 2006, at times there were only two people at the study although it averaged about six people. In 2008, this study averages fifteen people per week and has had a maximum of twenty-two. In addition, more members report they are reading their Bibles daily.

The most surprising increase came in giving of time, talent, and treasure. Before the jail churches began 52 percent agreed or strongly agreed that their giving was good. After the jail churches began, the percentage jumped to 79 percent. This is a net increase of 27 percent in members' perception of their giving. This is backed by the church records. The income for the mother church in 2006 was $92,208. The income in 2007 rose to $107,119. Income to date through July 2008 is $70,208 with projected annual income of $120,356. It appears that the jail churches have impacted the generosity of the members of Amazing Grace. The members are more willing to give because they see that the mother church is a church in mission.

Two of the main factors that have greatly increased in the mother church are prayer and a spirit of love. Before 2006, 60 percent of respondents agreed or strongly agreed that they practiced prayer regularly. After 2006, the number escalated to 84 percent. This is a net increase of 24 percent. However, increase in prayer is exceeded by the increase of the spirit of love. Before the jail churches, 67 percent of respondents felt they had a spirit of love. After the jail churches began, this already high number skyrockets to 94 percent. The members of the mother church comment on these two factors in Figure 7.

Figure 7. Responses that reflect increased prayer and a spirit of love

I keep this ministry in my prayers because I believe all of us have been touched by this. —Sandi

Transfer of love from inside the community to outside the community. Opened our eyes and our hearts to the hurting inmates and their families. Their prayers from jail seem to be for others. —Darol

I think it is giving the church a strong bond between the church and the Lord. —Anonymous

Keeps us realizing that all people need Christ in every aspect of their lives. —Bridget

I don't judge people as much. I tend to see that the people should get a second chance. —Li

Affects my prayer life. Every week my husband and I pray for all requests. Opened our hearts to embrace folks now out of jail non-judgmentally. —Glenda

I am more understanding with those who are caught in the judicial system. Whether the person is innocent or not, he or she deserves my love, compassion, and prayers. We are more loving and accepting of new people. Appearance and mode of dress are not a factor in how we welcome visitors to our worship. —Babbi

It is opening my heart and life to people in need, out of my normal circle. Also, I enjoy the prayer cards. —Teresa

It proves that you open your arms the way Jesus would want. You don't judge. Only love and happiness comes from within your walls. —Chrissy (new member)

It has affected our church on prayer, to pray for one, closeness, and obeying God, and how to forgive and not to judge. —Anonymous

The increase in the practice of prayer and the spirit of love at Amazing Grace has been phenomenal. The mother church planted churches with the plan of having inmates' lives transformed. In the process, the members have found their own lives transformed.

The Inmates' Responses

The responses of the inmates who became part of the jail churches have been encouraging. In response to the survey administered in July of 2008, eighty-eight members of the jail churches (out of about 150 who attend weekly) rated themselves in worship, Bible study, giving, prayer, and love.

The inmates' responses regarding worship demonstrate that 66 percent of the inmates agree or strongly agree that they have increased their worship practices while incarcerated. Two-thirds of the inmates have been touched by the Spirit through the jail churches. The comments from the inmates in Figure 8 demonstrate this point.

Figure 8. Responses that reflect increased worship attendance

---

Worship has brought peace to my life. —Anonymous

I can actually feel the Holy Spirit for the first time in my life. —Brian

Yes, jail church has worked wonders! We need more of it! —Richard

It feels like every time I get to church a big burden is lifted off my shoulders and I love it. —Anonymous

It has given me strength to cope with what I am going through in jail. It has also made me change my mind and turn to the Lord. I've started a new life and continue to follow the Lord. I realize the Lord is there for me. I always look forward to coming to the service. —Yolanda

Church has put joy in my heart! —Anonymous

Church is the only place that I can go to find a real smile and real caring. — Anonymous

---

> Church has been a blessing to all of us in here. It is giving me courage. —Anonymous

It is amazing how effective the jail churches have been in touching inmates' lives through worship. This has led the inmates to read and study their Bibles more. The surveys illustrated that 58 percent of inmates agree or strongly agree that jail church has increased their Bible reading habits. The inmates' comments regarding Bible reading and study are recorded in Figure 9.

Figure 9. Responses that reflect increased Bible study attendance

> Jail church has brought some hope to what is otherwise a very dismal place, and hopeless environment. It has brought me back to the word with more understanding. —Diana
>
> When the spirit gets weak, the Bible always has uplifting words of encouragement. —Traci
>
> Church has taught me to learn how to believe in the Lord, have faith, and to read the Bible. —Connie
>
> In the past eight and half months I have studied the Bible more than I ever had the in my twenty-five and a half years I have lived. —Jewel
>
> Church has brought me back to scripture. —David
>
> I am in Durango. I am reconciled with Christ. Now, I am preaching the word and everyone is accepting Christ. When I started there was seven. Now there is twenty eight. —Julio

Increased worship attendance and study of the word have led to generous giving among the inmates. The inmates can share their food and also the items they purchase with money their families or friends put on their books or accounts. This can include honey buns, cookies, toiletries, and the like. The survey shows that 57 percent of the inmates were more generous in their giving. The inmates comment on their own spirit of giving in Figure 10.

Figure 10. Responses that reflect increased giving

Jail church brought God and man together and saved souls. —Jewel

Church brings people together in a positive way. —Norma

It has brought light to a very dark world. —Barbara

Church has given the women that attend, a way to cope and get along with each other while we spend our days overcoming instances we've made for ourselves. —Traci

---

On many occasions the DOs have commented to the jail pastors that the jail churches have contributed to a better atmosphere in the pods. The evidence points to a more generous spirit between the inmates. This also includes the DOs who guard them.

The two areas of spirituality that had the largest percentage of increase were identical to the areas that increased in the mother church: prayer and the spirit of love. Astonishingly, seventy-two inmates either agreed or strongly agreed that the jail churches had increased their prayer lives and their spirit of love. The inmates clarify this in Figure 11.

Figure 11. Responses that reflect increased prayer and a spirit of love

Church gives us a feeling as a whole. There seems to be calmness over our pod afterwards. —Melissa

Church brings us together instead of against one another. —Angelique

Church has brought more girls closer together. —Sue

Church has brought a smile to some very unpleasant people. —Norma

Seeing things in different ways and seeing what prayers do. —Broderick

Church has affected me highly, mainly with the personal prayers and prayer requests. —Charles

I am praying for something. —Anonymous

Church has showed me that even in my darkest times; I can always talk and pray to God. —Christopher

Church has showed me how to ask Jesus into my life and how to pray. —Brian

I find myself talking to God more often than I used to. —Brent

The survey demonstrates that seven out of ten inmates have had the practice of prayer and the spirit of love increase in their lives. *These are inmates awaiting trial for assorted misdemeanors and felonies. They are people who have largely been self-centered until this point in their lives.* The changes in their lives are evidence of the effectiveness of jail churches but ultimately to the power of Jesus Christ to transform lives.

Number of New Jail Churches Planted

In 2006, Amazing Grace planted two jail churches at the Lower Buckeye jail and had two jail pastors. In 2007, another two jail churches were added at the Estrella jail for women and Amazing Grace had a total of four jail pastors. The jail pastors up to this point were all members of Amazing Grace. Unfortunately, one jail church was discontinued due to the jail pastor's health issues. The result was a total of three active jail churches.

In 2008, two more jail churches were added in Durango jail and at the time of this writing an additional church is planned for the fall of 2008. One of the new jail churches offers worship in Spanish. There are an additional three jail pastors. Two of these pastors are members of another inner-city congregation. By the end of 2008, the mother church will have planted six jail churches in three different jails with a total of seven jail pastors serving. Numerically, the jail planting efforts of Amazing Grace can be considered successful.

Cathy Gardner, the mother of a former inmate, sums up this attempt at evaluation and success with her extended comments:

The jail ministry saved my son's life and gave him back to me. I had prayed and prayed to God to find Michael. I didn't know my prayers would be answered in such a unique way. My son was arrested and taken to Lower Buckeye jail. Jail is not the place most moms want their sons to be and it was not my first choice either, but at least I knew where he was. So while God was getting Michael arrested, He was working on the hearts of some very special people at Amazing Grace church. These busy people with plenty of other ways to use their time stopped and listened to the call of the Holy Spirit. They became willing to help people society looks down on. They went into the jails, armed with love, which only God can provide, and ministered to those in such great need. My son has been touched in every possible way. He has been unconditionally accepted and lovingly reminded of who he is and more importantly whose he is. A miracle occurred in my son's life because people were willing to listen and to follow the Holy Spirit's call to serve. That would have been enough for me, but God in His love and mercy was not through. Seeing the radical change in our son brought his dad back to the Lord. He witnessed the love and acceptance of this congregation not only for our son but for himself! My husband and son are not the only people to undergo change as the result of the love of Amazing Grace church. I too have changed. I always thought of myself as a Christian with the love of Christ in my heart and a willingness to serve. But the first time I entered through those red doors to worship with my son, something happened to me. It was as if I had been worshipping with my eyes closed and now they are wide open. I too have been welcomed with the same love and acceptance that every person God leads to Amazing Grace church receives in abundance. The word of God is in action at Amazing Grace and miracles do happen, are happening because of this congregation and the willingness to do God's work. So absolutely, my life has been changed. When I am next to my husband worshipping and watching my son assisting in worship, my heart is full of love and gratitude. I give thanks to God for the open hearts of the jail pastors and the support of the congregation that made the commitment to serve in this mission of love.[3]

God has poured his grace in abundance into the Maricopa County jails through the jail churches planted by Amazing Grace Christian Church. Ironically, *this does not match the grace, mercy, and love which God has lavished upon the mother church*. The goodness of God in Jesus Christ is truly awesome!

CONCLUSION

The jail churches, just as any ministry to the incarcerated, are very precious to Jesus. This is reason enough to plant jail churches. However, in order to encourage the planting of jail churches, I have discovered there are seven reasons to plant jail churches. Some of these reasons have been adapted from Phil Van Auken, professor of management at Baylor University: to minister to the incarcerated is commanded by Jesus; the jails and prisons are America's most fertile soil for the gospel; the planting of jail churches breathes new life into the local church; the jail churches get members into the harvest field; the jail churches teach deep spiritual lessons; the jail churches produce new members for the local church; and ministry to the incarcerated is motivated out of a love for the lost.[1] These reasons surfaced in my research for this book and have been confirmed by my experience as a jail church planter and as pastor of the mother church.

Jesus has commanded his Church to visit those who are incarcerated. Schwarz declares, "Prison [jail] ministry has a direct scriptural mandate (Matt. 25: 31-40). Throughout the Bible are examples, descriptions, and commandments about prisons, prisoners, bondage, captivity, and slavery. The Bible mentions prison, prisoners, or imprisonment more than 130 times."[2] Those who are in jails and prisons are very important to Christ and he commands his Church to go to them. To neglect this charge is disobedient and has eternal ramifications according to Scripture. In the parable of the sheep and the goats, Jesus concludes, "Then they [those who neglected the incarcerated Christ] will go away to eternal punishment, but the righteous to eternal life" (Matt. 25: 46). It is time for the Church to obey and go.

Furthermore, as described in Chapter 3, the inmates are very fertile soil for the Gospel. The inmates are people who have tried everything possible to obtain what they considered "the good life" and have discovered they are in a hell hole. *In twelve years of pastoral ministry, I have never seen a group of people listen as intently to a sermon as the inmates in the jails.* They do not want to hear that they are all right and the world is beautiful. These lost souls want the truth. They have heard enough lies. Lies will not stop their hurting and empty hearts. The inmates are searching for an answer to fix their lives. They come to the jail churches hoping the jail pastors can give them the answer. The jail pastors do give them the answer, and his name is Jesus.

Planting jail churches also breathes new life into the mother church. The members of Amazing Grace are excited about the jail churches. *They realize that planting jail churches is a transformational ministry blessed by God.* The members see the change in the jail pastors, the inmates, the inmates' families, and in themselves. The members of Amazing Grace have become more loving, prayerful, and more missions oriented. The church is no longer circling the wagons in a survival mode. It has become more selfless and outward focused. Through this process the Holy Spirit has breathed new life into Amazing Grace.

In addition, the jail churches bring church members into the harvest field. The members are the future jail pastors. Within months after the first two jail churches were planted by Widney and me, three members of Amazing Grace inquired about becoming jail pastors. Two of these members have been faithfully serving as jail pastors over the past year. Moreover, when these jail pastors return from the mission field, they inspire others to become involved in mission. Since the jail churches began, Boy Scouts, Girl Scouts, and a Christian daycare have started at Amazing Grace. Putting people into the mission field makes mission contagious in the local church.

Also, the jail churches teach deep spiritual lessons to the mother church. *The spiritual lessons Amazing Grace has learned include: the importance of loving all people, of not being judgmental, being changed by the Spirit, being generous, being an open vessel, and being honest and open; the power of prayer; the truth that God is in charge; the need to look for Christ in all people and things; the need for Bible study; the blessings that come with taking risks; the blessings that come by being surprised by God; and the importance of simply going.* These truths were taught to the members of Amazing Grace by a spiritual osmosis. The truths surfaced in prayer requests, Bible studies, sermons, conversations, fellowship, worship, and prayer. As the pastor of the mother church, I would like to take credit but the Holy Spirit did all the teaching. Amazing Grace and I are just along for the ride and what a wild ride it is!

Another reason to plant jail churches is that it produces new members for the local church. It should not be expected that a great number of new members will join local churches due to a jail ministry, but a few passionate new believers are likely to come. The handful of new Christians Amazing Grace has received from the jails have brought their families and friends, but more importantly their enthusiasm. They are excited about Jesus and his Church. They want to tell everybody about Jesus and what he has done for them. *The released inmates and their families bring new life and passion to the mother church.* This passion affirms the mission of planting jail churches and it is also very contagious with the established members.

Most importantly, the main reason for the planting of jail churches is out of a love for the lost. The mother church will be blessed in numerous ways by planting jail churches. However, this cannot be one's motivation. John writes, "Whoever does not love does not know God, because God is love" (1 John 4:8). *The motivation for planting jail churches is love—love for God and love for others. If love is not the main focus in planting jail churches, then an individual or a church should not plant jail churches.* Repentance and getting the DNA right in the mother church should be the priority. When love, however, is the impetus behind planting jail churches, it takes the mother church and pastors on an exciting and transformational adventure.

When God started this adventure two years ago at Amazing Grace, I had no idea of the lives that would be changed by it. I expected some inmates to be changed by Jesus. I never anticipated, however, that their families, friends, the jail pastors, and the members of Amazing Grace would experience such a wonderful transformation. To my amazement, the transformation the Spirit has worked in me has been overwhelming and humbling. I pray that as others start the journey of church planting, they may also experience the power, the love, and the peace of Christ that Amazing Grace and I have experienced in planting churches in the Maricopa County jail complex. *"Now to him who is able to establish you by my gospel and the proclamation of Jesus Christ, according to the revelation of the mystery hidden for long ages past, but now revealed and made known through the prophetic writings by the command of the eternal God, so that all nations might believe and obey him—to the only wise God be glory forever through Jesus Christ! Amen"* (Rom. 16: 25-27).

APPENDIX A

Mission Statement, Core Values, and Vision of Amazing Grace Christian Church

Mission Statement

To love all people to Christ, by becoming Jesus' followers, and by enjoying the ever-changing adventure of Jesus.

Core Values

The church's core values are: Christ alone (John 14:6), love (Matt. 22:37-38), community (John 13:34-35), evangelism/all-inclusiveness (Matt. 28:18-20), prayer (Matt. 21:22), discipleship (Matt. 16:24), authority of Scripture (2 Tim. 3:16-17), freedom to be who we are in Christ (John 8:36), and hope (Rom. 15:13).

Vision

We will be a growing and changing community in Christ, reaching out in love to all people, and free to risk all in serving Christ.

APPENDIX B

EVALUATION FORM

(Administered to the members of Amazing Grace Christian Church)

PLEASE CIRCLE ONLY ONE NUMBER. Please circle 1 if you strongly disagree or circle 5 if you strongly agree. Circle 2 if you simply disagree or circle 4 if you simply agree. Circle 3 for neutral or no change.
Please answer honestly.

Before 2006, when we began the jail ministry, please rank yourself in the following factors.

1. **Worship Attendance:**

    Strongly Disagree   1   2   3   4   5   Strongly Agree

2. **Bible Study Attendance:**

    Strongly Disagree   1   2   3   4   5   Strongly Agree

3. **Giving of my Time, Talent, and Treasure:**

    Strongly Disagree   1   2   3   4   5   Strongly Agree

4. Practice of Prayer:

Strongly Disagree   1   2   3   4   5   Strongly Agree

5. Spirit of Love:

Strongly Disagree   1   2   3   4   5   Strongly Agree

After 2006, when we began the jail ministry, please rank yourself in the following factors:

6. Worship Attendance:

Strongly Disagree   1   2   3   4   5   Strongly Agree

7. Bible Study Attendance:

Strongly Disagree   1   2   3   4   5   Strongly Agree

8. Giving of my Time, Talent, and Treasure:

Strongly Disagree   1   2   3   4   5   Strongly Agree

9. Practice of Prayer:

Strongly Disagree   1   2   3   4   5   Strongly Agree

10. Spirit of Love:

Strongly Disagree   1   2   3   4   5   Strongly Agree

Has the jail ministry affected you in any specific ways? If so, how?

How do you think our jail ministry has affected our church?

**First Name Only
(Optional):**_____

APPENDIX C

EVALUATION FORM

(Administered to the inmates who have attended a jail church)

PLEASE CIRCLE ONLY ONE NUMBER. Please circle 1 if you strongly disagree or circle 5 if you strongly agree. Circle 2 if you simply disagree or circle 4 if you simply agree. Circle 3 for neutral or no change.
Please answer honestly.

After attending the jail church, please rank yourself in the following factors:

1.   Worship Attendance:

Strongly Disagree   1   2   3   4   5   Strongly Agree

2.   Bible Study Attendance:

Strongly Disagree   1   2   3   4   5   Strongly Agree

3.   Giving of my Time, Talent, and Treasure:

Strongly Disagree   1   2   3   4   5   Strongly Agree

4.   **Practice of Prayer:**

       Strongly Disagree   1   2   3   4   5   Strongly Agree

5.   **Spirit of Love:**

       Strongly Disagree   1   2   3   4   5   Strongly Agree

Has the jail church affected you in any specific ways? If so, how?

**First Name Only
(Optional):**_____

APPENDIX D

NECESSARY STEPS TO BEGIN JAIL MINISTRY

1. Prayer for discernment, empowerment and the harvest.
2. Form leadership team.
3. Select jail pastors.
4. Train and equip jail pastors.
5. Contact the sheriff or head chaplain.
6. Fill out required paperwork for church and volunteers.
7. Work with chaplain and jail pastor regarding time and place of service.
8. Get jail pastors trained, fingerprinted, and obtain badges.
9. Inspect facility with chaplain before the first service.
10. Spend at least one month training jail pastor at the new jail church. Employ "show-how" training.
11. Let jail pastor take over jail church responsibilities.
12. Meet once a month with jail pastors for debriefing and support.

NOTES

Introduction

[1]William Easum and Thomas G. Bandy, *Growing Spiritual Redwoods* (Nashville: Abingdon Press, 1977), 177.
[2]This information was provided to me in personal conversations with several inmates at the Lower Buckeye jail.
[3]Richard Shaw, *Chaplains to the Imprisoned* (New York: Haworth Press, 1995), 151.
[4]Duane Peterson, quoted in Shaw, *Chaplains to the Imprisoned*, 151.
[5]Shaw, *Chaplains to the Imprisoned*, 70.
[6]Lennie Spitale, *Prison Ministry: Understanding Prison Culture Inside and Out* (Nashville: Broadman and Holman Publishers, 2002), 263.
[7]W. Thomas Beckner and Jeff Park, *Effective Jail and Prison Ministry for the Twenty-First Century* (Charlotte, NC: A Coalition of Prison Evangelists Publication, 1998), 69.
[8]Ibid., 11.
[9]Henry G.Covert, *Ministry to the Incarcerated* (Chicago: Loyola Press, 1995), 116.
[10]Eddie Gibbs, *In Name Only* (Downers Grove, IL: InterVarsity Press, 1994), 100.

Chapter 1

[1]Timothy F. Lull, *Martin Luther's Basic Theological Writings* (Minneapolis, MN: Fortress Press, 1989), 480-481.
[2]Leonard Sweet, *Aqua Church* (Loveland, CO: Group Publishing, 1999), 103.
[3]Mike Regele and Mark Schultz, *Death of the Church* (Grand Rapids: Zondervan Publishing House, 1995), 96-97.
[4]Steve Goodwin, "Turn-Around Churches," DMin class, Fuller Theological Seminary, Pasadena, CA, January 5-16, 2004.

[5]Paul G. Hiebert, "The Gospel in our Culture: Methods of Social and Cultural Analysis," in George R. Hunsberger and Craig Van Gelder, eds., *The Church between Gospel and Culture: The Emerging Mission in North America* (Grand Rapids: William B. Eerdmans Publishing Company, 1996), 156.

[6]Rodney Clapp, *A Peculiar People: The Church as Culture in a Post-Christian Society* (Downers Grove, IL: InterVarsity Press, 1996), 19.

[7]Martin Luther, quoted in Hunsberger and Van Gelder, *The Church between Gospel and Culture*, 199.

[8]Lyle E. Schaller, *The New Reformation: Tomorrow Arrived Today* (Nashville: Abingdon Press, 1995), 13.

[9]Regele and Schultz, *Death of the Church*, 205.

[10]Raymond S. Rosales, *It's about Mission! Ventures and Views of a Pilgrim in Hispanic Ministry* (St. Louis, MO: Concordia Publishing House, 1998), 116-117.

[11]Robert E. Logan and Neil Cole, *Beyond Church Planting* (St. Charles, IL: ChurchSmart Resources, 2005), 128.

[12]Statement made to me personally by council president Melvin Norton, June 3, 2003.

[13]Peter M. Senge, *The Fifth Discipline Fieldbook* (New York: Doubleday, 1994), 302.

[14]Chuck Smith, Jr., *The End of the World . . . As We Know It* (Colorado Springs, CO: WaterBrook Press, 2001), 197.

[15]"The City of Glendale," http://www.glendaleaz.com/1-, 3-, 5-, 10-mile radius demographics (accessed January 26, 2002). Information is based on the 2000 census report.

[16]Ibid.

[17]Ibid.

[18]Bob Schwarz, *You Came unto Me: A Training Manual for Jail and Prison Ministry* (Colorado Springs, CO: Harvestime International Network, 1998), 65.

[19]Joseph M. Arpaio, *America's Toughest Sheriff* (Arlington, TX: Summit Publishing House, 1996), 76.

[20]Henry G. Covert, *Ministry to the Incarcerated* (Chicago: Loyola Press, 1995), 49-50.

[21]Amazing Grace Christian Church baptismal records.

[22]Regele and Schultz, *The Death of the Church*, 175.

[23]Ibid., 164.

[24]John Fischer, *12 Steps for the Recovering Pharisee (Like Me)* (Minneapolis, MN: Bethany Publishing House, 2000), 49.

[25]Cursillo literally means "a short course." It is a three-day retreat that is a short course in Christianity. Cursillo is a great discipleship program and in many cases life changing. Equivalent movements are Walk to Emmaus, *Tres Dias*, and *Via De Cristo*.

[26]Alpha is a discipleship program, consisting of fifteen taped sessions and study materials, created by the Reverend Nicky Gumbel.

[27]My estimation after serving as pastor for the past six years.

[28]Fischer, *12 Steps for the Recovering Pharisee*, 70.
[29]Erwin R. McManus, *An Unstoppable Force* (Loveland, CO: Group Publishing, 2001), 168.
[30]Sweet, *AquaChurch*, 191-192.
[31]William Easum, *Sacred Cows Make Gourmet Burgers: Ministry Anytime, Anywhere by Anyone* (Nashville: Abingdon Press, 1995), 9.
[32]Covert, *Ministry to the Incarcerated*, 90.
[33]Schwarz, *You Came unto Me*, 83.
[34]Beckner and Park, *Effective Jail and Prison Ministry*, ix.

Chapter 2

[1]Chaplain Gregory Millard, speech given at an annual training class at the jail complex in October 2006.
[2]Arpaio, *America's Toughest Sheriff*, 41.
[3]Ibid., 51.
[4]Covert, *Ministry to the Incarcerated*, 5.
[5]Arpaio, *America's Toughest Sheriff*, 232.
[6]Ibid., 14.
[7]Chaplain Gregory Millard, speech given at an annual training class at the jail complex in October 2006.
[8]Arpaio, *America's Toughest Sheriff*, 69.
[9]Spitale, *Prison Ministry*, 95.
[10]Ibid., x–xi.
[11]Covert, *Ministry to the Incarcerated*, 34.
[12]Ibid., 38-39.
[13]Ibid., 20.
[14]Ibid., 41.
[15]Kelly Preiss, personal interview with the author at the Lower Buckeye jail in March 2006.
[16]Erica, personal interview with the author at Amazing Grace in September 2007.
[17]Spitale, *Prison Ministry*, 115.
[18]Schwarz, *You Came unto Me*, 79.
[19]Ibid., 83.
[20]Chaplain Gregory Millard, speech given at an annual training class at the jail complex in October 2006.
[21]Arpaio, *America's Toughest Sheriff*, 155.
[22]Covert, *Ministry to the Incarcerated*, 9.
[23]Ibid., 16.
[24]Ibid., 17.
[25]Ibid., 47.
[26]Ibid., 27.
[27]Schwarz, *You Came unto Me*, 7.
[28]Ibid., 44.

[29]Covert, *Ministry to the Incarcerated*, 29.

[30]Ibid., 30.

[31]Beckner and Park, *Effective Jail and Prison Ministry*, 18.

[32]Spitale, *Prison Ministry*, 6-7.

[33]Schwarz, *You Came unto Me*, 45.

[34]Beckner and Park, *Effective Jail and Prison Ministry*, 182.

[35]Schwarz, *You Came unto Me*, 70.

[36]Beckner and Park, *Effective Jail and Prison Ministry*, 159.

[37]Ibid., 159.

[38]Shaw, *Chaplains to the Imprisoned*, 45.

Chapter 3

[1]George Hunsberger, "The Newbigin Gauntlet: Developing a Domestic Missiology for North America," in Hunsberger and Van Gelder, *The Church between Gospel and Culture*, 14-15.

[2]Chaplain Millard stated this fact at the annual jail volunteer orientation.

[3]Shaw, *Chaplains to the Imprisoned*, 47.

[4]Ibid., 48.

[5]Beckner and Park, *Effective Jail and Prison Ministry*, 103.

[6]This information has been gathered based on several informal conversations I have had with inmates within the Maricopa jails.

[7]Gibbs, *In Name Only*, 21.

[8]Dallas Willard, *The Great Omission* (San Francisco: Harper San Francisco, 2006), xii.

[9]Ibid., xii.

[10]Ibid., 71.

[11]Glen H. Stassen, *Authentic Transformation* (Nashville: Abingdon Press, 1996), 140.

[12]George G. Hunter, III, *Church for the Unchurched* (Nashville: Abingdon, 1996), 47.

[13]Covert, *Ministry to the Incarcerated*, 93.

[14]Logan and Cole, *Beyond Church Planting*, 44.

[15]Spitale, *Prison Ministry*, 20.

[16]Ibid., 190.

[17]Lull, *Martin Luther's Basic Theological Writings*, 31.

[18]Stassen, *Authentic Transformation*, 179.

[19]Beckner and Park, *Effective Jail and Prison Ministry*, 168.

[20]Bill Yount, *I Heard Heaven Proclaim* (Hagerstown, MD: McDougal Publishing, 2004), 50-52.

[21]Stassen, *Authentic Transformation*, 186.

[22]Eddie Gibbs, *Church Next: Quantum Changes in How We Do Ministry* (Downers Grove, IL: InterVarsity Press, 2000), 155.

[23]Walter C. Hobbs, "Dependence on the Holy Spirit," in *Treasures in Clay Jars*, ed. by Lois Y. Barrett (Grand Rapids: William B. Eerdmans Publishing Company, 2004), 119.

[24]Stassen, *Authentic Transformation*, 167.

[25]Covert, *Ministry to the Incarcerated*, 88.

[26]Ibid., 91-92.

[27]Fischer, *12 Steps for the Recovering Pharisee*, 69.

Chapter 4

[1]Os Guinness, *Dining with the Devil: The Megachurch Movement Flirts with Modernity* (Grand Rapids: Baker Book House, 1993), 39.

[2]Easum, *Sacred Cows Make Gourmet Burgers*, 45-46.

[3]George Hunsberger, "Sizing up the Shape of the Church," in Hunsberger and Van Gelder, *The Church between Gospel and Culture*, 337.

[4]Spitale, *Prison Ministry*, 86-87.

[5]Easum, *Dancing with Dinosaurs–Ministry in a Hostile Environment* (Nashville: Abingdon Press, 1993), 19.

[6]Schwarz, *You Came unto Me*, 48.

[7]Easum, *Dancing with Dinosaurs*, 73.

[8]Robert Logan and Neil Cole, *Raising Leaders for the Harvest* (St. Charles, IL: ChurchSmart Resources, 1995), 2-3.

[9]Logan and Cole, *Beyond Church Planting*, 15.

[10]Ibid., 6.

[11]Robert Logan, *Be Fruitful and Multiply* (St. Charles, IL: ChurchSmart Resources, 2006), 17.

[12]Logan and Cole, *Beyond Church Planting*, 5.

[13]Ibid., 6.

[14]Roland Allen, quoted in Logan and Cole, *Raising Leaders for the Harvest*, 3-13.

[15]Logan and Cole, *Beyond Church Planting*, 3.

[16]Class notes for the DMin course, "Missional Church Planting," with Bob Logan, Fuller Theological Seminary, Pasadena, CA, July 10-14, 2006.

[17]Spitale, *Prison Ministry*, 87.

[18]Class notes for the DMin course, "Missional Church Planting," with Bob Logan, Fuller Theological Seminary, Pasadena, CA, July 10-14, 2006.

[19]Logan and Cole, *Beyond Church Planting*, 45.

[20]Beckner and Park, *Effective Jail and Prison Ministry*, 98.

[21]Logan and Cole, *Raising Leaders for the Harvest*, 6-22.

[22]Logan and Cole, *Beyond Church Planting*, 5.

[23]Ibid., 75.

[24]Ibid., 61.

[25]Logan and Cole, *Raising Leaders for the Harvest*, 3-11.

[26]Ibid., 3-21.

[27]Spitale, *Prison Ministry*, 195.

[28]Logan and Cole, *Beyond Church Planting*, 21.

[29]Spitale, *Prison Ministry*, 83.

[30]Logan and Cole, *Beyond Church Planting*, 20.

[31]Logan and Cole, *Raising Leaders for the Harvest*, 6-8.

[32]Logan and Cole, *Beyond Church Planting*, 118.

[33]Joseph M. Arpaio, *Custody Support Division Handbook* (Phoenix, AZ: Maricopa County Sheriff's Office, 2006), 31.

[34]Logan and Cole, *Beyond Church Planting*, 47.

[35]Covert, *Ministry to the Incarcerated*, 88.

[36]Spitale, *Prison Ministry*, 58-59.

[37]Logan and Cole, *Raising Leaders for the Harvest*, 3-5.

[38]Hunter, *Church for the Unchurched*, 166.

[39]Logan, *Be Fruitful and Multiply*, 41.

[40]Class notes for the DMin course, "Missional Church Planting," with Bob Logan, Fuller Theological Seminary, Pasadena, CA, July 10-14, 2006.

[41]Covert, *Ministry to the Incarcerated*, 77.

[42]Logan and Cole, *Beyond Church Planting*, 23.

[43]Logan and Cole, *Raising Leaders for the Harvest*, 2-17.

[44]Shaw, *Chaplains to the Imprisoned*, 48.

[45]Sherwood G. Lingenfelter and Marvin K Mayers, *Ministering Cross-Culturally: An Incarnational Model for Personal Relationships* (Grand Rapids: Baker, 2003), 17.

Chapter 5

[1]Jonathan Edwards, quoted by Logan and Cole, *Raising Leaders for the Harvest*, 2-6.

[2]Jim Cymbala, *Fresh Wind, Fresh Fire* (Grand Rapids: Zondervan Publishing House, 1997), 53.

[3]Ibid., 57.

[4]Schwarz, *You Came unto Me*, 14.

[5]Cymbala, *Fresh Wind, Fresh Fire*, 182.

[6]At the time of this writing, two of the Durango jail churches have been launched and the third is due to be launched at the end of 2008.

[7]Jaime's last name is fictional in order to preserve his anonymity.

[8]Logan and Cole, *Beyond Church Planting*, 31-36.

[9]Gordon T. Smith, *Listening to God* (Downers Grove, IL: InterVarsity Press, 1997), 9.

[10]Logan, *Be Fruitful and Multiply*, 48.

[11]Smith, *Listening to God*, 25.

[12]Ibid., 28.

[13]Ignatius Loyola, quoted by Gordon T. Smith, *The Voice of Jesus* (Downers Grove, IL: InterVarsity Press, 2003), 41.

[14]Smith, *Listening to God*, 53.

[15]Ibid.
[16]Smith, *The Voice of Jesus*, 31.
[17]Smith, *Listening to God*, 48.
[18]Ibid., 41.
[19]Ibid., 48.
[20]Ibid., 128.
[21]Ibid., 52.
[22]Smith, *The Voice of Jesus*, 227.
[23]Spitale, *Prison Ministry*, xiv.
[24]Henri Nouwen, *In the Name of Jesus* (New York: Crossroad Publishing Company, 1989), 37-38.
[25]Logan, *Be Fruitful and Multiply*, 112.
[26]Ibid.
[27]Beckner and Park, 63.
[28]Logan and Cole, *Beyond Church Planting*, 79.
[29]See the section titled "Prayer Cover (Intercessors): Inside and Outside" earlier in this chapter.
[30]Logan and Cole, *Raising Leaders for the Harvest*, 3-11.
[31]This will be discussed in greater detail in Chapter 6.
[32]Logan and Cole, *Raising Leaders for the Harvest*, 6-2.
[33]I was first introduced to CoachNet in Logan's Missional Church Planting course.
[34]Logan, *Be Fruitful and Multiply*, 100.

Chapter 6

[1]Logan and Cole, *Raising Leaders for the Harvest*, 2-4.
[3]E.M. Bounds, quoted by Logan and Cole, *Raising Leaders for the Harvest*, 1-29.
[3]Logan and Cole, *Raising Leaders for the Harvest*, 68.
[4]Ibid., 73.
[5]Logan and Cole, *Beyond Church Planting*, 19.
[6]Ibid., 19.
[7]Spitale, *Prison Ministry*, 245.
[8]Covert, *Ministry to the Incarcerated*, 82.
[9]Spitale, *Prison Ministry*, 227.
[10]Ibid., 195.
[11]Van Gelder, "Defining the Center – Finding the Boundaries," in Hunsberger and Van Gelder, *The Church between Gospel and Culture*, 32.
[12]Fischer, *12 Steps for the Recovering Pharisee*, 124.
[13]Clapp, *A Peculiar People*, 167.
[14]Beckner and Park, *Effective Jail and Prison Ministry*, 26.
[15]Logan, *Be Fruitful and Multiply*, 57.
[16]See Chapter 7 for a thorough discussion of results.

[17]Beckner and Park, *Effective Jail and Prison Ministry*, 22.
[18]Ibid., 23.
[19]Schwarz, *You Came unto Me*, 5.
[20]Covert, *Ministry to the Incarcerated*, 81.
[21]Ibid., 116.
[22]Shaw, *Chaplains to the Imprisoned*, 59.
[23]Ibid., 61.
[24]Ibid., 58.
[25]Covert, *Ministry to the Incarcerated*, 4.
[26]Spitale, *Prison Ministry*, 29.
[27]Fischer, *12 Steps for the Recovering Pharisee*, 95.
[28]Letter from Cathy Gardner, received by the author, July 20, 2006.
[29]"Witness talks" are personal testimonies of how Jesus Christ has impacted a person's life and transformed the individual.
[30]Beckner and Park, *Effective Jail and Prison Ministry*, 98.
[31]Fischer, *12 Steps for the Recovering Pharisee*, 112.
[32]Ibid., 126.
[33]Beckner and Park, *Effective Jail and Prison Ministry*, 95.
[34]Covert, *Ministry to the Incarcerated*, 116-117.
[35]Clapp, *A Peculiar People*, 89.
[36]Covert, *Ministry to the Incarcerated*, 117.
[37]Gibbs, *Church Next*, 177-178.

Chapter 7

[1]Schwarz, *You Came unto Me*, 84.
[2]Shaw, *Chaplains to the Imprisoned*, 141.
[3]Letter from Cathy Gardner, received by the author, July 20, 2006.

Conclusion

[1]Phil Van Auken, Baylor University professor of management, from an article found on his website, *Ten Ways Prison Ministry Promotes Church Growth*.
[2]Schwarz, *You Came unto Me*, 7.

BIBLIOGRAPHY

Abraham, William J. *The Logic of Renewal*. Grand Rapids: William B. Eerdmans Publishing Company, 2003.

Allen, Roland. *Paul's Missionary Methods: St. Paul's or Ours?* Grand Rapids: William B. Eerdmans Publishing Company, 1983.

Allen, Roland. *The Spontaneous Expansion of the Church*. Grand Rapids: William B. Eerdmans Publishing Company, 1962.

Arpaio, Joseph M. *America's Toughest Sheriff*. Arlington, TX: Summit Publishing House, 1996.

Arpaio, Joseph M. *Custody Support Division Handbook*. Phoenix, AZ: Maricopa County Sheriff's Office, 2006.

Barna, George. *The Turn-Around Church*. Ventura, CA: Regal Books, 1993.

Barrett, Lois Y., Darrel L. Guder, Walter C. Hobbs, George R. Hunsberger, Lindford L. Stutzman, Jeff Van Kooten, and Dale A. Ziemer. *Treasures in Clay Jars*. Grand Rapids, MI: William B. Eerdmans Publishing Company, 2004.

Beckner, W. Thomas and Jeff Park. *Effective Jail and Prison Ministry for the Twenty-First Century*. Charlotte, NC: A Coalition of Prison Evangelists Publication, 1998.

Bosch, David Jacobus. *Transforming Mission*. Maryknoll, NY: Orbis Books, 1991.

Clapp, Rodney. *A Peculiar People: The Church as Culture in a Post-Christian Society*. Downers Grove, IL: InterVarsity Press, 1996.

Covert, Henry G. *Ministry to the Incarcerated*. Chicago: Loyola Press, 1995.

Cymbala, Jim. *Fresh Wind, Fresh Fire*. Grand Rapids: Zondervan Publishing House, 1997.

Easum, William. *Dancing with Dinosaurs—Ministry in a Hostile Environment*. Nashville: Abingdon Press, 1993.

_____. *Leadership on the Other Side: No Rules, Just Clues*. Nashville: Abingdon Press, 2000.

_____. *Sacred Cows Make Gourmet Burgers: Ministry Anytime, Anywhere by Anyone*. Nashville: Abingdon Press, 1995.

Easum, William and Thomas G. Bandy. *Growing Spiritual Redwoods*. Nashville: Abingdon Press, 1997.

Fischer, John. *12 Steps for the Recovering Pharisee (Like Me)*. Minneapolis: Bethany Publishing House, 2000.

Gibbs, Eddie. *Church Next: Quantum Changes in How We Do Ministry*. Downers Grove, IL: InterVarsity Press, 2000.

_____. *In Name Only*. Downers Grove, IL: InterVarsity Press, 1994.

Goodwin, Steven J. *Catching the Next Wave: Leadership Strategies for Turn-Around Congregations.* Minneapolis: Augsburg Publishing House, 1999.

Guinness, Os. *Dining with the Devil: The Megachurch Movement Flirts with Modernity.* Grand Rapids: Baker Book House, 1993.

Hunsberger, George R. and Craig Van Gelder, eds. *Church between Gospel and Culture: The Emerging Mission in North America.* Grand Rapids: William B. Eerdmans Publishing Company, 1996.

Hunter, George G., III. *Church for the Unchurched.* Nashville: Abingdon Press, 1996.

Hybels, Bill and Mark Mittelberg. *Becoming a Contagious Christian.* Grand Rapids: Zondervan Publishing House, 1994.

Johnson, Luke. *Scripture and Discernment: Decision Making in the Church.* Nashville: Abingdon Press, 1996.

Lingenfelter, Sherwood G. and Marvin K. Mayers. *Ministering Cross-Culturally: An Incarnational Model for Personal Relationships.* Grand Rapids: Baker Book House, 2003.

Logan, Robert E. *Be Fruitful and Multiply.* St. Charles, IL: ChurchSmart Resources, 2006.

Logan, Robert E. and Neil Cole. *Beyond Church Planting.* St. Charles, IL: ChurchSmart Resources, 2005.

Logan, Robert E. and Neil Cole. *Raising Leaders for the Harvest.* St. Charles, IL: ChurchSmart Resources, 1995.

Lull, Timothy F. *Martin Luther's Basic Theological Writings.* Minneapolis: Fortress Press, 1989.

McManus, Erwin R. *An Unstoppable Force*. Loveland, CO: Group
   Publishing, 2001.

Mead, Loren. *The Once and Future Church: Reinventing the
   Congregation for a New Mission Frontier*. Herndon, VA:
   Alban Institute, 1991.

Moorman, David. *Harvest Waiting*. St. Louis: Concordia Publishing
   House, 1993.

Nolan, Pat. *When Prisoners Return*. Merrifield, VA: Prison
   Fellowship, 2004.

Nouwen, Henri. *In the Name of Jesus*. New York: Crossroad
   Publishing Company, 1989.

Regele, Mike and Mark Schultz. *Death of the Church*. Grand Rapids:
   Zondervan Publishing House, 1995.

Rosales, Raymond S. *It's about Mission! Ventures and Views of a
   Pilgrim in Hispanic Ministry*. St. Louis: Concordia Publishing
   House, 1998.

Schaller, Lyle E. *Discontinuity and Hope: Radical Change and the
   Path to the Future*. Nashville: Abingdon Press, 1999.

Schaller, Lyle E. *The New Reformation: Tomorrow Arrived Today*.
   Nashville: Abingdon Press, 1995.

Schwarz, Bob. *You Came unto Me: A Training Manual for Jail
   and Prison Ministry*. Colorado Springs, CO: Harvestime
   International Network, 1998.

Senge, Peter M. *The Fifth Discipline Fieldbook*. New York:
   Doubleday, 1994.

Shaw, Richard. *Chaplains to the Imprisoned.* New York: Haworth Press, 1995.

Smith, Chuck, Jr. *The End of the World...As We Know It.* Colorado Springs, CO: WaterBrook Press, 2001.

Smith, Gordon T. *Listening to God.* Downers Grove, IL: InterVarsity Press, 1997.

_____. *The Voice of Jesus.* Downers Grove, IL: InterVarsity Press, 2003.

Spitale, Lennie. *Prison Ministry: Understanding Prison Culture Inside and Out.* Nashville: Broadman and Holman Publishers, 2002.

Stassen, Glen H. *Authentic Transformation.* Nashville: Abingdon Press, 1996.

Sweet, Leonard. *Aqua Church: Essential Leadership Arts for Piloting Your Church in Today's Fluid Culture.* Loveland, CO: Group Publishing, 1999.

Warren, Rick. *The Purpose Driven Church.* Grand Rapids: Zondervan Publishing House, 1995.

Willard, Dallas. *The Great Omission.* San Francisco: Harper San Francisco, 2006.

_____. *Renovation of the Heart: Putting on the Character of Christ.* Colorado Springs, CO: NavPress, 2002

Wright, Tim. *Unfinished Evangelism.* Minneapolis: Augsburg Publishing House, 1995.

Yount, Bill. *I Heard Heaven Proclaim.* Hagerstown, MD: McDougal Publishing, 2004.

CPSIA information can be obtained at www.ICGtesting.com
Printed in the USA
LVOW121409110313

323699LV00001B/38/P